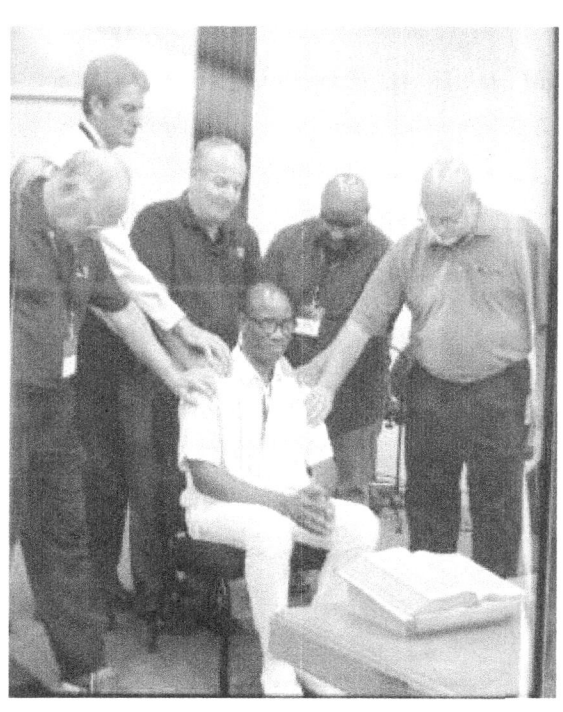

Authentic Spiritual Values

Authentic Spiritual Values

Authentic Spirituality Group

Authentic Spiritual Values

Copyright (c) 2024 by Atinsola N.O

ISBN: 979-889480729-4 - Soft Cover

ALL RIGHTS RESERVED

No part of this publication may be reproduced, stored in an electronic system, or transmitted in form by any means electronics, mechanical, photocopying, recording, or otherwise without permission of the permission of the author, Brief quotations may be used in literary criticism.

FOR INFORMATION CONTACT

Deacon Atinsola N.O, (Houston, Texas)
Email: Najeem.atinsola@yahoo.com,
authenticspiritualvalue@gmail.com.
Book Printed in U.S.A, Amazon.com, Inc Digital

Prayer

Heavenly Father, as your word said in 1Peter 4:10, *"Each of you should use whatever gift you have received to serve others as faithful stewards of God's grace in its various forms"*; we come with humble hearts, seeking wisdom and guidance as we open the pages of the book "Authentic Spiritual Values," a profound source of inspiration and guidance, inspired by Matthew 23:25-27. May love illuminate our minds and stir our spirits.

Lord, help us to see beyond the external forms of piety and religious duty to the more profound call of genuine discipleship. Teach us to value the purity of our hearts over the appearances we maintain before others. May Your Spirit, our guide and revealer, convict us of hypocrisy where it exists within us and lead us into a life of greater authenticity and holiness.

Grant us the courage to face the uncomfortable truths about ourselves and the grace to change. Help us not to just understand, but embody the principles of justice, mercy, and faithfulness that Your Son, Jesus, exemplified. Let this exploration not only increase our understanding but transform our actions.

Let us cherish this transformative journey through the book, not as a mere source of information, but as a profound catalyst for change. May we not just be hearers of Your Word, but doers; not just outwardly compliant, but inwardly renewed.

We thank You for the opportunity to grow closer to You through these teachings. May Your wisdom guide us, your truth free us and Your love inspire us as we earnestly seek to live authentically in Your sight.

In Jesus' name we pray. Amen.

Preface

"Authentic Spiritual Values"

The depths of Matthew 23:25-27" is a book that takes readers on a transformative journey. It delves into the profound wisdom embedded within the scripture, offering a unique approach that beckons readers towards genuine spiritual enlightenment, drawing inspiration from Matthew 23:25-27. The book's exploration of the timeless teachings of Jesus Christ distinguishes it, guiding readers toward a deeper understanding of authentic spirituality.

Rooted in a unique approach to biblical scholarship, the exploration of Matthew 23:25-27 is enhanced by references to other relevant scriptures, such as Psalm 51:10 and Proverbs 4:23. These biblical insights serve as pillars, bolstering the book's central theme of cultivating genuine spiritual values in a world often consumed by superficiality.

"Exploring Authentic Spiritual Values" integrates perspectives from renowned spiritual thinkers like Thomas Merton. Drawing from Merton's works, the book offers practical wisdom and guidance, empowering readers with the tools they need to navigate the complexities of modern life while staying rooted in timeless spiritual principles. The integration of diverse perspectives enriches the book's content, providing readers with a comprehensive understanding of authentic spirituality.

"Exploring Authentic Spiritual Values" is not a book of the past but a relevant guide for today. Through thought-provoking reflections, insightful commentary, and practical applications, it serves as a roadmap for individuals seeking to deepen their spiritual lives and align their values with the profound truths illuminated in Matthew 23:25-27. Whether you are a seasoned seeker or embarking on the path of spiritual exploration for the first time, this book offers guidance, inspiration, and transformative insights to illuminate your journey toward authentic spirituality.

Foreword

It is with profound gratitude and a deep sense of responsibility, as a spiritual leader and scholar, that I present "Authentic Spiritual Values," a book that endeavors to explore the essence of true spirituality as modeled by Jesus Christ. This journey through the teachings of Matthew 23:25-27 is not merely an academic exercise; it is a call to a transformative way of living that aligns our inner beliefs with our outward actions.

In a world increasingly dominated by superficial expressions of faith, such as attending religious services without true devotion, and where spirituality often succumbs to the pressures of public validation, such as posting about religious activities on social media for validation, rather than private conviction, this book aims to steer the conversation back to what matters most—the heart and soul of biblical teaching. The scriptures remind us that genuine spiritual vitality is borne out of authenticity, not merely adherence to religious norms.

"Authentic Spiritual Values" seeks to unveil the often overlooked but crucial aspects of Christ's teachings on hypocrisy and authenticity. It is divided into three parts: Part One explores the concept of hypocrisy and its implications in our spiritual lives; Part Two delves into the teachings of Jesus on authenticity and its transformative power; and Part Three offers practical guidance on how to live out these values in our daily lives. This book challenges each of us to reflect deeply on our own spiritual lives and to question whether we, like the Pharisees, are guilty of cleaning the outside of the cup while neglecting the interior. It offers a clarion call to embrace a holistic spirituality that encompasses a rigorous examination of our inner lives, urging us to prioritize personal transformation over public perception.

As we navigate through these pages, we will encounter the harsh but healing words of Christ, who did not hesitate to challenge the status quo of His time, such as His rebuke of the Pharisees' hypocrisy. We will be prompted to consider our spiritual practices: are they mere performances, or are they the genuine expressions of a heart changed by grace?

This book is not intended for the faint-hearted but for those empowered enough to dismantle the façade and dare to embrace a life of genuine faith. It is for those eager to build their spiritual lives with stones of tradition and the bedrock of transformation.

I am deeply thankful to the scholars, pastors, and everyday believers who have contributed their insights to this work. Their perspectives and experiences enrich our understanding and offer practical applications that bridge the gap between ancient texts and contemporary life.

May "Authentic Spiritual Values" serve as a guidepost, leading us toward a deeper, more authentic relationship with God. Let it be a tool that informs, inspires, corrects, and comforts as we seek to live out the values that Christ Himself embodied.

In this journey of discovery and renewal, may you find the courage to confront your spiritual realities and the strength to align them more closely with the values of the Kingdom of God.

With hope and prayer for your transformative journey,

Dr. Fasanya (Pastor)

RCCG Sufficient Grace Chapel

Prologue

In a world where materialism and surface appearances reign supreme, the quest for genuine spirituality is becoming increasingly crucial. The Book of Matthew, chapter 23, verse 25, offers a profound message from Jesus Christ that highlights the importance of true internal moral goodness over outward religiosity. 'Authentic Spiritual Values Matthew: 23:25' is a thought-provoking exploration of this message, urging readers to reflect on their spiritual journey.

This book goes beyond a mere examination of biblical texts. It is a compelling call to scrutinize our lives through the lens of authentic spiritual values. By analyzing Matthew 23:25 in-depth and exploring its historical context, theological significance, and modern-day implications, this work presents a comprehensive view of living a life that genuinely reflects our deepest beliefs and virtues.

Through its pages, readers embark on a journey to understand Jesus Christ's message in Matthew 23:25 and how it applies to our lives today. The author emphasizes prioritizing internal moral goodness over outward religiosity and how such values can help us achieve spiritual fulfillment. This book is a must-read for anyone seeking to live a meaningful life that reflects their profound beliefs and virtues.

Biography

Najeem O. Atinsola is an ordained Deacon minister and Christian wedding officiant known for his profound understanding of biblical teachings and impressive academic background, bringing his unique blend of spirituality and love to each ceremony. He is a doctoral degree student studying Clinical Psychology (with a focus on mental health). He is a Divinity Student at the Christian Leader Institute.

Najeem's passion for the practical application of spiritual teachings has not only earned him numerous ministry awards, including the Bible Study Award, Bible Interpretation Award, Restoration Connection Award, Prayer Ministry Award, and more, but also serves as a powerful testament to his unwavering commitment to faith and relentless pursuit of knowledge, inspiring others to follow in his footsteps.

In his latest book, 'Authentic Spiritual Values Matthew: 23:25,' Najeem Atinsola not only continues to inspire and educate readers on the importance of embracing a life of authenticity and moral integrity but also provides practical guidance on how to do so. This insightful work offers a comprehensive analysis of Matthew 23:25 and its spiritual values, empowering readers to apply them to their daily lives. Najeem's unique perspective and extensive biblical knowledge make this book an invaluable resource for anyone seeking to deepen their understanding of spirituality and lead a more fulfilling life.

> *_"For this very reason, make every effort to add to your faith goodness; and to goodness, knowledge; and to knowledge, self-control; and to self-control, perseverance; and to perseverance, godliness; and to godliness, mutual affection; and to mutual affection, love. For if you possess these qualities in increasing measure, they will keep you from being ineffective and unproductive in your knowledge of our Lord Jesus Christ."*
> 2 Peter 1:5-8 (NIV)

Authentic Spiritual Values

Author's Note

Dear reader,

It is with great humility that I present my book, "Authentic Spiritual Values Matthew 23:25." This work offers a unique perspective on spiritual authenticity, born from years of personal reflection and a deep study of Jesus Christ's teachings, particularly His admonitions against hypocrisy in Matthew 23.

Today, what we often see in the church is a form of Christianity that I refer to as 'Synthetic Christianity'; this mindset is where believers align themselves with Christian traditions, values, and practices yet lack a personal commitment to faith. It's a type of nominal Christianity, where adherence to cultural norms precedes genuine belief and relationship with God. In the Bible, Jesus cautions against this superficial faith in Matthew 15:8-9, quoting Isaiah: 'These people honor me with their lips, but their hearts are far from me.'

The Bible outlines that today, what we often see in the church is a form of Christianity that some authors have termed 'Synthetic Christianity.' In this state, believers align themselves with Christian traditions, values, and practices yet lack a personal commitment to faith. It's a type of nominal Christianity, where adherence to cultural norms precedes genuine belief and relationship with God.

In the Bible, Jesus cautions against this superficial faith in Matthew 15:8-9, quoting Isaiah: *"These people honor me with their lips, but their hearts are far from me."* The Bible outlines the characteristics of synthetic Christianity, which include attending church for social reasons rather than spiritual growth (Hebrews 10:25), engaging in religious rituals without understanding their significance (Isaiah 29:13), and prioritizing worldly pursuits over spiritual matters (Matthew 6:24). It's a matter of outward conformity without inner transformation, as warned in Romans 12:2: "Do not conform to the pattern of this world but be transformed by the renewing of your mind." characteristics of synthetic Christianity, which include attending church for social reasons rather than spiritual growth (Hebrews 10:25), engaging in religious rituals without understanding their significance (Isaiah 29:13), and prioritizing worldly pursuits over spiritual matters (Matthew 6:24).

It's a matter of outward conformity without inner transformation, as warned in Romans 12:2: *'Do not conform to the pattern of this world but be transformed by the renewing of your mind.'*

My aim is not just to provide a deeper understanding of this verse, but to ignite a spark of personal growth and transformation within you. This book is a guide for anyone seeking to enrich their spiritual life, to live their faith with integrity and sincerity, and to embark on a journey of self-discovery and authenticity.

I warmly invite you to engage with this work, approaching it with an open mind and heart. Let's explore how ancient wisdom can guide us toward a more fulfilling and authentic life.

Let's embark on this journey of discovering genuine spiritual values together.

Acknowledgements

This book has been a transformative journey of personal and spiritual discovery, a path illuminated by the grace of Almighty God and His Son, Jesus Christ. The Holy Spirit has guided me as I painstakingly crafted each page. I am also deeply grateful to the many individuals who have walked this path with me, offering their support and contributing their unique insights.

I want to express my deepest gratitude to my family, who have been my constant source of strength and inspiration. My wife, Elizabeth, has been exceptionally patient and understanding in supporting me throughout this journey. My children, Oluwa Damilare, Diana, and Genevieve, have also been an inspiration and a reminder of the values that I strive to embody in this work.

I owe a debt of gratitude to my academic mentors, Pastor DR. A.R. Bernard (Christian Cultural Center, Brooklyn, NY.), Pastor DR. Okonrende (RCCG Pavilion of Redemption, Houston, TX.), and the entire team of the Christian Leaders Institute (CLI). Their rigorous training and thoughtful guidance have helped shape my approach to scripture and this work. Special thanks to Pastor Dr. Bankole Fasanya (RCCG Sufficient Grace Chapel, Indianapolis) and Rev. Dr. O VGeart, whose insights into spiritual guardians and biblical input have been invaluable.

My colleagues and fellow ministers at RCCG, Pavilion of Redemption, deserve special recognition for their stimulating discussions and camaraderie, which have enriched this book.

Their perspectives and critiques have challenged me and deepened my understanding of the vast landscape of spiritual values.

I am also grateful to the members of my congregation whose real-life stories and experiences, shared with such honesty and faith, have provided both inspiration and grounding for the concepts discussed in this book.

I want to acknowledge the instrumental role of my editor, Rev. Dr. O Vgeart, and the publishing team at Amazon, whose patience, keen eye, and commitment to literature have significantly enhanced the final product's quality, making it a true reflection of our collective efforts.

Lastly, I am profoundly thankful to God, whose teachings inspire and form the very foundation of all I write and do. This book is a testament to the grace I have received and the divine wisdom that guides us all, a wisdom that has touched each of us in unique and profound ways.

I sincerely thank everyone who has contributed to this meaningful endeavor.

Authentic Spiritual Values

Table of Contents

Prayer..3

Preface... 4-5

Forward 6-8

Prologue...9

Biography...10-11

Author's Note..12-13

Acknowledgments.. 14

Table of Contents....................................... 15-17

Introduction: 18-20

Chapter One
Exploring Authentic Spiritual Values........................ 21-22

Chapter Two
Contextual Background of Matthew 23:25 23-29

Chapter Three
Unveiling Hypocrisy and Authenticity 30-33

Chapter Four
Spiritual Values vs. External Appearances................. 34-45

Chapter Five
The Heart of Authenticity: Integrity and Sincerity......... 46-65

Chapter Six
Overcoming Hypocrisy: Practical Steps for
Spiritual Growth 66-117

Chapter Seven
Cultivating Authentic Spiritual Values
in Daily Life.. 118-121

Chapter Eight
The Transformative Power of Authenticity in
Relationships 122-135

Chapter Nine
Lessons from Jesus' Teachings on Authenticity............ 136-142

Chapter Ten
Reflections on Personal Authenticity and
Spiritual development...143-149

Chapter Eleven
Conclusion: Embracing Authenticity in
Pursuit of Spiritual Wholeness 150-151

Chapter Twelve
Overcoming Hypocrisy:
The Salvation Vs Cathedral (FIG REE) 152

Chapter Thirteen
References and Further Study................................ 153-158

Introduction

True Authenticity

A potter named Eliab lived in the small village of Eshel, surrounded by olive groves and the distant murmur of the sea. Eliab was known for his skillful hands, which shaped clay into beautiful vessels, and his profound spiritual wisdom.

One day, a young Jotham, his heart heavy with the weight of his father's expectations, found himself at Eliab's workshop. As Eliab prepared his clay for the next creation, Jotham's mind was a storm of conflicting desires and societal norms, a battle that left him in a state of profound inner turmoil.

"Master Eliab," Jotham began hesitantly, his voice filled with hope and uncertainty. "Everyone expects me to take over my father's business, but my heart longs to study the scriptures and serve our community." His eyes filled with compassion, Eliab nodded and gestured for Jotham to continue.

Eliab listened intently, nodding. He took a lump of clay and handed it to Jotham. "Shape this into what you desire," he instructed.

Jotham's hands were clumsy; the clay fell apart under his uncertain touch. Frustrated, he looked up at Eliab. "I cannot do it. It does not hold together," he admitted.

Eliab's eyes sparkled with a wisdom that seemed to transcend time as he took the clay back. "Jotham, like this clay, your spirit needs shaping. Authentic spiritual values are not inherited or imposed;

they are deeply personal and must be shaped by one's own hands." His words, laden with years of wisdom and patience, carried the promise of a transformative journey.

He began to knead the clay, his fingers working methodically. "See, each vessel I create must first undergo the fire to gain strength and durability. Similarly, to be good, one must undergo trials and listen to one's inner voice to discover one's true path."

Moved by Eliab's words, Jotham spent many days in the potter's workshop, learning the art of pottery and meditating on his beliefs and desires. With each vessel he shaped, he felt his purpose becoming clearer. He realized that his journey in pottery reflected his spiritual journey, requiring patience, perseverance, and a deep understanding of oneself. He faced trials of self-doubt, societal pressure, and fear of failure. But each trial, like the fire that strengthens the vessel, only made him more resilient and determined, realizing this caused a significant turning point in his life, inspiring hope for personal growth.

Months passed, and the village celebrated the festival of harvest, a time of abundance and gratitude. The festival was a cherished tradition, symbolizing the community's connection to the land and their shared prosperity. Jotham presented his father with a set of vessels, each adorned with verses from the scriptures. His father was deeply touched, seeing the genuine joy in his son's eyes and understanding the profound meaning behind the gift during this festive season.

"I have watched you these past months, my son," his father said. "And I see that your spirit has found its calling not in commerce but in community and faith."

With his father's blessing, Jotham became a revered teacher, using the lessons he learned from clay and fire to guide others. He taught that actual spiritual value lies in authenticity and personal conviction, much like the vessels he once shaped—each unique, each firm in its form. His teachings resonated with the community, sparking a wave of inspiration that led many to embark on their journeys of self-discovery and personal growth.

In Eshel, Eliab's workshop remained a place where many came to learn about shaping clay and soul, a testament to the enduring power of authentic spiritual values. The workshop, with its humble tools and the echo of Eliab's teachings, stood as a symbol of the transformative journey each person could undertake, a reminder that the pursuit of authenticity and personal growth is a lifelong endeavor. The workshop was a simple structure, its walls adorned with pots of various shapes and sizes, each a testament to the transformative power of the potter's hands and the clay's resilience.

Chapter One

"Exploring Authentic Spiritual Values"

"Woe to you, teachers of the law and Pharisees, you hypocrites! You clean the outside of the cup and dish, but inside, they are full of greed and self-indulgence. [26] Blind Pharisee! First, clean the inside of the cup and dish, and then the outside will be clean.
Matthew 23:25

Jesus uses a metaphor to criticize the Pharisees for their hypocrisy. He compares them to whitewashed tombs that appear beautiful and clean on the outside but are full of dead men's bones and uncleanness on the inside. This passage highlights the importance of inner purity over outward appearances.

In today's world, Matthew 23 will remind the Church of God that the Church is more concerned about physical structures than soul-gaining for God. Jesus cautions against prioritizing grandiose buildings and material wealth over genuine spiritual growth and service to others. Instead of focusing on extravagant structures; Jesus teaches the importance of humility, sincerity, and compassion. This aligns with the biblical message of caring for the poor and marginalized rather than pursuing wealth and power.

In Matthew 6:24, Jesus explicitly states, *"No one can serve two masters. Either you will hate and love or be devoted*

to and despise the other. You cannot serve both God and money."

Pursuing financial gain should not overshadow one's devotion to God and Jesus's teachings.

Matthew 23:25 reminds us not to focus too much on external appearances and material possessions. Instead, our priority should be cultivating inner purity and genuine spiritual values like kindness, compassion, and humility.

These qualities make us genuinely righteous in God's eyes and enable us to live out Jesus' teachings daily by following Jesus' example and prioritizing our inner selves, we can become more like him and positively impact the world.

Rather than just going through the motions of religious rituals; we can embody the true spirit of Christianity by loving God with all our hearts, souls, and minds and loving our neighbor as ourselves.

Let us heed Jesus' warning and focus on what truly matters - our inner selves and our relationships with others. In doing so, we can become beacons of light and love in a world that desperately needs it.

Chapter Two

Contextual Background
"Authentic Spiritual Values"
Matthew 23:25

Historical and Cultural Context

The "Seven Woes" chapter in the Gospel of Matthew powerfully reminds us that true righteousness comes from the heart, not outward appearances. Jesus condemns the hypocrisy of the Pharisees and law teachers, urging us to live authentically and sincerely. Written by Matthew the Apostle for a Jewish audience, this chapter takes place in the final days leading up to Jesus' crucifixion in Jerusalem. Let us all strive to live honestly and honestly, following Jesus's example.

"Woe to you, teachers of the law and Pharisees, you hypocrites! You clean the outside of the cup and dish, but inside, they are full of greed and self-indulgence."
Matthew 23:25

This metaphor highlights the contrast between external religious appearances and internal moral decay.

Theological Context

The Pharisees, a prominent religious group in Judaism, were known for their strict observance of the Torah. However, Jesus criticizes them for their observance and lack of genuine heart transformation. The verse calls for introspection and proper spiritual cleanliness, which resonates with themes found in other biblical texts.

Internal vs. External Righteousness
"But those things which proceed out of the mouth come forth from the heart, defiling the man"
Matthew 15:18

In Matthew 15:18, Jesus teaches that what comes out of the mouth proceeds from the heart-this defiles a person; the focus of the Church is to redirect people to God and not turn their minds away from them.

Hypocrisy and Authentic Faith

Luke 11:39 and Matthew 23:25 inspire us with the importance of inner purity. These verses remind us that: True beauty lies within; we must cultivate our inner selves rather than just our external appearances. Let us strive to follow Jesus' teachings and purify our hearts and minds to radiate goodness and light to the world around us.

And the Lord said unto him, "Now do ye Pharisees clean the outside of the cup and the platter; but your inward part is full of ravening and wickedness."
Luke 11:39

Literary Context
The book of Matthew 23 is structured around a series of "woes" that serve as a literary device to pronounce judgment. This declaration represents a prophetic and mirrors Old Testament

prophetic books that often-declared woes against various sins of Israel and other nations (e.g. Isaiah and Ezekiel) when people were stepping outside the way of their God.

Immediate Context

"Woe to you, teachers of the law and Pharisees, you hypocrites! You give a tenth of your spices—mint, dill, and cumin—but you have neglected the rest essential matters of the law—justice, mercy, and faithfulness. It would be best to practice the latter without neglecting the former. 24 You blind guides! You strain out a gnat but swallow a camel".
Matthew 23:23-24

In Matthew 23-24, Jesus teaches us a powerful lesson about what true righteousness entails. He reminds us that while it's important to give back, we must always remember the weightier matters of the law, such as justice, mercy, and faithfulness. He urges us to focus on internal righteousness rather than just external appearances, for what's on the inside counts. Let us always strive for a pure and sincere heart and lead a life full of kindness and compassion towards others.

Interpretative Analysis

For if any be a hearer of the word and not a doer, he is like unto a man beholding his natural face in a glass: For he beholdeth himself, and goeth his way, and straightway forgetteth what manner of man he was.
James 1:23-24

Authentic Spiritual Values

The Pharisees of Jesus' time were known for their strict adherence to the Torah. They were considered the most devout and learned religious leaders of their day. However, Jesus criticized them for their rigid observance of the law and lack of genuine heart transformation. According to Jesus, they were more concerned with following the letter of the law than cultivating a relationship with God and living a life of love and service to others.

This verse calls for introspection and proper spiritual cleanliness. It reminds us that spiritual growth is not just about following rules and regulations but developing a deep and sincere relationship with God. It challenges us to reflect on the disparity between external religious observance and internal moral and spiritual states.

The Book of James also addresses this issue, urging us to be doers of the word and not just hearers (James 1:22). It challenges us to examine our hearts and lives to see whether our faith is genuine and producing fruit. The verse warns against the dangers of hypocrisy, where leaders enforce strict rules on others but fail to apply spiritual principles in their own lives.

The message reminds us of the importance of focusing on spiritual development rather than the external trappings of religion. It reminds us that the church is not just a physical building or a set of rituals, but a community of believers called to love and serve one another. What the church is witnessing now can be related to James 1:23-24, which discusses a person who looks at his face in a mirror and forgets what he looks like. This means that some of our church leaders practiced self-deception in spiritual practices to lure people away from self-awareness and genuine spiritual transformation. As believers, we must be vigilant against this deception and strive to live out our faith sincerely and authentically.

Application to Modern Readers

Matthew 23:25, one of the chapters in the Bible's New Testament, emphasizes the importance of examining one's spiritual life beyond surface-level religiosity. The chapter encourages modern believers to look past the external appearance of religious observance to delve deeper into their motives and actions. By doing so, one can ensure that they align with the biblical principles of integrity and authenticity.

Reflecting on one's spiritual life is crucial for growing as a believer. Regularly assessing one's motives and actions helps to ensure that one's religious observance is not just external but is also reflected in one's internal morals and Spiritual states. This practice challenges the reader to reflect on the disparity between external religious observance and internal spiritual states.

It also serves as a cautionary tale that warns against hypocrisy, where leaders enforce strict rules on others but fail to apply spiritual principles in their lives. In essence, Matthew 23:25 encourages believers to examine their spiritual lives regularly, beyond surface-level religiosity, to ensure they live authentic and integrated lives that align with biblical principles of integrity and authenticity.

Authentic Spiritual Values

> **"Woe to you, teachers of the law and Pharisees, you hypocrites! You clean the outside of the cup and dish, but inside, they are full of greed and self-indulgence"**
> Matthew 23:25

Community Accountability emphasizes the importance of living and engaging with a body of Christ community where honesty, vulnerability, and mutual support is valued, it involves engaging in community life, sharing experiences and helping each other grow in true spiritual maturity. This approach is based on the belief that we are not meant to live in isolation but rather in a community where we can learn from each other's experiences and support one another in our spiritual journey.

One key aspect of Community Accountability is a sincere examination of one's spiritual life beyond surface-level religiosity. It requires regularly assessing one's motives and actions to ensure they align with biblical principles of integrity and authenticity; it goes beyond performing religious rituals and traditions and instead focusing on cultivating an inner life that reflects the teachings of Jesus Christ.

Matthew 23:25 is a critical verse for understanding the difference between mere religious formalism and genuine faith. Jesus rebukes the Pharisees for their hypocrisy, pointing out that they focus on external appearances while neglecting the state of their hearts. This verse is a timeless reminder of the importance of cultivating an inner life that reflects the teachings of Jesus Christ and ensuring that outward religious expressions are grounded in true spiritual transformation.

Authentic Spiritual Values

By exploring the themes of Community Accountability and Authentic Spiritual Values, we can deepen our understanding of what it means to have a genuine and transformative faith. This exploration not only enriches our spiritual journey but also allows us to contribute to the growth and well-being of our community.

Chapter Three

(Unveiling Hypocrisy and Authenticity)

"Woe to you, teachers of the law and Pharisees, you hypocrites! You are like whitewashed tombs, which look beautiful on the outside but are full of the bones of the dead and everything unclean on the inside. 28 In the same way, on the outside, you appear to people as righteous but, on the inside, you are full of hypocrisy and wickedness".
Matthew 23:27-28

The chapter "Unveiling Hypocrisy and Authenticity" is a thought-provoking exploration of the significance of genuine spiritual transformation in the teachings of Jesus Christ. The author provides a comprehensive interpretation of Matthew 23:25-27, which includes an insightful historical analysis of the Pharisaic system and its emphasis on ritual purity, a practice that Jesus firmly renounced. Furthermore, the text refers to Matthew 7:21-23 as another example of how the outward appearance of religiosity can be misleading. Jesus talks about those who perform miracles in his name but do not know him.

The importance of these teachings in the lives of contemporary spiritual practitioners is that the modern Christians can easily fall into the trap of focusing on outward appearances and adhering to religious rituals rather than genuinely transforming their hearts and minds. This issue is particularly relevant in today's era, where social media often promotes an idealized spiritual life, which can lead to the loss of authenticity and sincerity. The text explores the enduring significance of Jesus' teachings in our modern era. It urges readers to wholeheartedly welcome genuine personal growth and sincerity as they navigate their spiritual paths.

> *"A person is not a Jew who is one only outwardly, nor is circumcision merely outward and physical. ²⁹ No, a person is a Jew who is one inwardly; and circumcision is circumcision of the heart, by the Spirit"*
> Romans 2: 28-29

This analysis builds upon the teachings of the Bible and emphasizes the significance of internal righteousness over external religiosity. The book of Romans, specifically chapter 2, verses 28-29, highlights the importance of being a Jew inwardly, with the circumcision of the heart by the Spirit rather than by the letter. True righteousness comes from within and cannot be achieved solely through external practices.

Similarly, Luke 11:39-41 echoes the same message, where Jesus admonishes the Pharisees for their emphasis on ritual cleanliness while neglecting justice and the love of God. This highlights that a person's outward display of religious practices is not as important as their internal state of being and their actions towards others.

The true righteousness comes from within and through the guidance of the Holy Spirit. Simply performing external rituals is not enough; one must also address the state of one's heart and how one treats others.

> *"Those who consider themselves religious and yet do not keep a tight rein on their tongues deceive themselves, and their religion is worthless."*
> James 1:26

Another lesson from the verse is warning against performing religious duties to gain the attention and admiration of others. It stresses the importance of being sincere in one's relationship with God. James 1:26 mentions that merely performing religious practices without being mindful of one's speech and thoughts is futile. The verse links genuine religiosity with ethical living, implying that true spirituality is not limited to external practices but is reflected in one's inner life.

While encourages readers to apply these biblical insights to their daily lives, it emphasizes that spiritual authenticity is not a one-time event but involves a continual process of self-examination by aligning one's inner life with outward expressions of faith. The challenge is maintaining integrity in both private and public spheres of life.

In other word, true spirituality is involves ensuring that our spiritual practices are not merely for show but reflect a deeply rooted faith, and believers must strive to live a life of honesty and transparency, where their actions align with their beliefs.

Authentic Spiritual Values

> ***Then the Lord said to him, "Now then, you Pharisees clean the outside of the cup and dish, but inside you are full of greed and wickedness. [40] You foolish people! Did not the one who made the outside also make the inside? [41] But now, as for what is inside you—be generous to the poor, and everything will be clean for you".***
> Luke 11:39-41

"Unveiling Hypocrisy and Authenticity" this is a concept of genuine spiritual transformation and its need in today's world for understanding and applying critical spiritual principles, emphasizing the importance of authenticity and sincerity in one's spiritual journey.

The bible is skillful bridges and ancient biblical wisdom with contemporary challenges, providing the believers with a timeless guide for pursuing authentic spiritual values.

The book of Bible offers practical insights and advice on overcoming hypocrisy and cultivating genuine spirituality, growth, highlighting the importance of self-awareness, humility, and compassion.

Whether you are a spiritual seeker, a religious scholar, or someone looking to deepen your understanding of spirituality, bible lesson "Unveiling Hypocrisy and Authenticity" offers a profound and insightful exploration of the human condition and the universal quest for meaning and purpose.

Authentic Spiritual Values

Chapter Four

Spiritual Values vs. External Appearances

Throughout our existence, we face the challenge of finding a balance between our spiritual values and the external appearances we project to the world. This struggle is not new, as it has been present throughout human history and reflected in the teachings of various religious traditions.

Let us deeply dive into this timeless theme, drawing insights from biblical wisdom and contemporary perspectives. Through exploration and reflection, we aim to provide a nuanced understanding of this dynamic's complexities and offer valuable guidance on cultivating authenticity and integrity through God's teachings.

> *"When they had finished eating, Jesus said to Simon Peter, "Simon son of John, do you love me more than these?" "Yes, Lord," he said, "you know I love you." Jesus said, "Feed my lambs."*
> John 21:15

Setting the Stag

> *"Those who want to get rich fall into temptation, a trap, and many foolish and harmful desires that plunge people into ruin and destruction. [10] For the love of money is the root of all kinds of evil. Some people, eager for money, have wandered from the faith and pierced themselves with many griefs"*.
> 1 Timothy 6:9.

The human experience is a complex journey that seeks meaning, purpose, and fulfillment. Questions of identity, values, and beliefs often guide this journey. When individuals seek spiritual growth and enlightenment, they frequently encounter conflicting messages and expectations internally and externally. The tension between spiritual values, which are rooted in inner convictions, moral principles, and external appearances, which are shaped by societal norms and expectations can present a significant challenge.

To navigate these challenges, Christians must understand their fleshly desires and submit to God's voice and direction. It means recognizing and acknowledging their weaknesses, limitations, and strengths. It includes being aware of the societal pressures that can lead them astray from their spiritual path.

In essence, achieving spiritual growth and enlightenment requires a deep understanding of oneself and a willingness to follow the guidance of a higher power. It is a journey that requires introspection, self-reflection, and a commitment to living a life guided by inner convictions and morals.

> *Again, Jesus said, "Simon, son of John, do you love me?" He answered, "Yes, Lord, you know that I love you." Jesus said, "Take care of my sheep." 17 The third time he said to him, "Simon son of John, do you love me?" Peter was hurt because Jesus asked him the third time, "Do you love me?" He said, "Lord, you know all things; you know that I love you." Jesus said, "Feed my sheep".*
> John 21:16-18

Biblical Insights

The Gospel of Matthew, 23: 25-27, is pivotal in Jesus Christ's life. It captures his courageous confrontation with the religious leaders of his time, the scribes, and Pharisees. In this encounter, he exposes their hypocritical behaviors and advocates for a shift towards internal renewal rather than a mere display of external righteousness.

Jesus's message was clear and powerful. He pointed out the scribes and Pharisees' preoccupation with superficialities, like washing the outside of a cup, while neglecting the inside, symbolizing their true selves. His call was for a reversal of priorities, urging them to focus on purifying their inner beings before attending to external appearances. Jesus emphasized that this was more important than religious rituals and traditions.

This timeless message resonates even today, as some religious leaders place undue emphasis on external appearances of the Church and material possessions, such as the grandeur of their church auditoriums, rather than internal transformation. However, Jesus reminds us that true righteousness emanates from within.

Through internal renewal, we can evolve into better versions of ourselves and positively influence the world.

> *"Whoever loves money never has enough; whoever loves wealth is always dissatisfied with their income. This, too, is meaningless"*.
> Ecclesiastes 5:10

Authentic Spiritual Values

In one of Jesus's teachings, He used a powerful metaphor to expose the hypocrisy of the scribes and Pharisees. He likened them to cups and dishes that were meticulously cleansed on the outside but filled with greed and self-indulgence on the inside. This metaphorical comparison highlights the danger of prioritizing outward appearances over inner transformation and authenticity.

Jesus urged the scribes and Pharisees to cleanse the inside of the cup first, emphasizing the importance of inner transformation as the foundation for genuine righteousness. This message reminds us that true righteousness comes from a pure heart and a sincere desire to do what is right rather than from performing external acts of righteousness for show.

Jesus compared the scribes and Pharisees to whitewashed tombs, which were beautiful on the outside but filled with decay and uncleanness. This vivid imagery further emphasizes the danger of hypocrisy and the spiritual decay that arises when appearances are prioritized over authenticity. Using these metaphors, Jesus challenges us to look beyond appearances and focus on the inner transformation, which is necessary for true righteousness, it calls us to seek authenticity in all aspects of our lives and to prioritize inner purity over external displays of righteousness.

Interpreting the Passage

Matthew 23:25-27 contains a profound message that offers a valuable insight into the nature of true spirituality and the dangers of superficiality. The passage challenges us to prioritize inner integrity and authenticity over shallow displays of righteousness. Jesus' message encourages us to examine our motives and intentions, ensuring that our actions align with our inner values and beliefs and that we are not merely seeking to conform to external standards.

The cup and dish metaphor used in the passage reminds us that true righteousness originates from within the heart. Simply following religious rituals and standards is insufficient; it requires a deep and sincere commitment to moral and ethical principles. This challenges us to cultivate a vibrant inner life characterized by love, compassion, and humility and to act accordingly. Similarly, the imagery of the whitewashed tombs serves as a warning against hypocrisy and the dangers of prioritizing image over substance. Spirituality cannot be faked or manufactured, and authenticity requires transparency and honesty, even when it exposes our vulnerabilities and shortcomings. Therefore, we must strive to be true to ourselves and others by living a life of integrity and sincerity.

Contemporary Reflections: Relevance Today

The passage from Matthew 23:25-27 was initially meant as a rebuke to the leaders and teachers of the old, who were more concerned with outward appearances and maintaining a particular image rather than genuine righteousness.

However, the message Jesus conveyed through this passage has a timeless relevance beyond that specific historical context.

Authentic Spiritual Values

In today's world, where social media and digital platforms have become ubiquitous and often shape our perceptions of ourselves and others, the pressure to maintain a particular image or persona can be overwhelming. We may feel compelled to present a specific version of ourselves, carefully curated and crafted to project success, popularity, or other desirable traits, this pressure to maintain appearances can come at the expense of our authenticity and genuine connection with others.

Jesus' message reminds us of the importance of focusing on inner righteousness and cultivating an authentic relationship with God rather than being overly concerned with outward appearances and the opinions of others. This way, we can find true fulfillment and meaning in life rather than constantly striving to live up to an impossible ideal.

> *"No one can serve two masters.*
> *Either you will hate the one and love the other, or you will be devoted to the one and despise.*
> *the other. You cannot serve God and money".*
> Matthew 6:24

Many people find it challenging to align their innermost values and beliefs with the expectations and pressures imposed on them by society. They may feel a strong urge to project a personal success, happiness, and fulfillment, even if it contradicts their authentic selves. This sense of disconnection between who they indeed are and who they portray themselves to be can often result in feelings of isolation, anxiety, and a sense of spiritual emptiness. An insightful father in the Lord once said "every person desires to be the best, which can lead to become greedy and chase worldly desires, losing sight of their true purpose and values".

Strategies for Cultivating Authenticity

The Bible is rich in teachings that guide believers in navigating the temptations and challenges of life. These teachings offer wisdom on remaining grounded in one's faith despite life's many distractions and obstacles. Similarly, the Bible guides how to manage the tension between one's spiritual values and the external appearances often valued by society.

One passage that offers insight on this topic is Matthew 23:25-27. In this passage, Jesus criticizes the Pharisees for focusing on external appearances rather than internal righteousness. He warns them that they are like "whitewashed tombs," beautiful on the outside but full of dead bones and uncleanness on the inside. This passage encourages believers to develop inner qualities, such as humility, love, and compassion, rather than simply trying to appear righteous to others.

In addition to these Biblical teachings, contemporary insights can be valuable in helping believers navigate the tension between spiritual values and external appearances for example, psychologists have found that focusing on internal values and goals rather than external validation can lead to greater happiness and well-being.

Authentic Spiritual Values

Drawing from Biblical wisdom and modern insights, believers can develop a deeper understanding of living a fulfilling and spiritually grounded life.

> ***Jesus left the temple and walked away when his disciples approached him to call his attention to its buildings. ² "Do you see all these things?" he asked. "Truly, I tell you, not one stone here will be left on another; everyone will be thrown down."***
> Matthew 24:1-2

Taking time for self-reflection can be a powerful tool in clarifying our values, beliefs, and motivations. By examining what truly matters to us, we can better understand what drives our actions and decisions. It's essential to consider what we're willing to stand for, even when it requires going against the grain. This can help us to maintain our integrity and stay true to ourselves.

Authenticity is another crucial aspect of leading a fulfilling life. Embracing our true selves and flaws can allow us to connect more deeply with ourselves and others. It can be tempting to conform to societal expectations or to present a false image of perfection, but this can ultimately lead to feelings of disconnection and emptiness. Instead, we should be vulnerable and authentic in our interactions with others can help us to build deeper, more meaningful relationships based on trust and mutual understanding.

Authentic Spiritual Values

> *"The words of the Teacher,[a] son of David, king in Jerusalem: "Meaningless! Meaningless!" Says the Teacher. "Utterly meaningless!*
> *Everything is meaningless."*
> Ecclesiastes 1:1-2

Integrity is a crucial aspect of life that should never be compromised, to live with integrity, we must align our actions with our values and let our words and deeds reflect our principles, it means being honest and truthful in everything.

We create a community when we surround ourselves with supportive individuals who value authenticity, fosters growth and personal development. Building meaningful relationships based on trust, respect, and mutual understanding is essential in cultivating a sense of belonging and purpose. It allows us to be ourselves and encourages us to be true to ourselves.

Let us strive to live with integrity and surround ourselves with a community that supports us in our journey toward becoming the best version of ourselves.

> *"What do people gain from all their labors*
> *At which they toil under the sun?*
> *⁴ Generations come, and generations go,*
> *But the earth remains forever.*
> *⁵ The sun rises, and the sun sets,*
> *And hurries back to where it rises.*
> *⁶ The wind blows to the south*

and turns to the north;
Round and round it goes,
ever returning on its course".
Ecclesiastes 1:3-6

The message conveyed in the text is about extending grace to oneself and others by recognizing that authenticity is a journey that involves moments of doubt, struggle, and growth. It emphasizes the importance of being kind to oneself and offering compassion to those on their paths of self-discovery. This means that we should strive to treat ourselves with the same love and kindness that we would offer to a dear friend or family member.

We must acknowledge that the journey towards self-discovery is not easy and that we will face challenges along the way however, extending grace to ourselves and others can help us stay positive and motivated and ultimately lead us toward a more fulfilling life. So, let us embrace our imperfections, learn from our mistakes, and extend kindness and compassion to ourselves and those around us.

"All streams flow into the sea, yet the sea
is never complete. To the place the streams
come from, there they return".
Ecclesiastes 1:7

Embracing Authenticity

One of the most significant challenges individuals face in their quest for meaning and fulfillment is the tension between their spiritual values and the external appearances they present to

Authentic Spiritual Values

the world. This dilemma has persisted throughout human history, transcending cultural and religious boundaries. However, the teachings Jesus offers timeless wisdom that can help us navigate this dynamic.

In Matthew 23:25-27, Jesus speaks of the importance of inner integrity and authenticity, reminding us that the purity of the inside is more important than the external appearances we present to others. He urges us to cultivate love, compassion, and humility-based spirituality. These are values that are universal and can be embraced by people of all faiths and belief systems.

As we strive to live out these teachings, we must resist the allure of superficiality and embrace the beauty of our true selves. This requires us to be honest with ourselves about our strengths and weaknesses and to be willing to share our vulnerabilities with others.

It also means extending grace to others, recognizing that authenticity is a journey of self-discovery and growth. The tension between spiritual values and external appearances is a challenge we all face. However, by following Jesus' teachings and cultivating a spirituality rooted in love, compassion, and humility, we can overcome this challenge and live more authentic, fulfilling lives.

"All things are wearisome, More than one can say. The eye never has enough of seeing, Nor the ear it's full of hearing".
Ecclesiastes 1:8

Authentic Spiritual Values

In the grand scheme of things, our worth as individuals is not dependent on the superficial indicators of achievement or the opinions of others but rather on the inner workings of our being and the genuineness of our motives. As we endeavor to create meaningful and significant lives, it is crucial to remember the teachings of Jesus Christ, who reminds us that true fulfillment comes not from external validation but from the unshakeable foundation of a virtuous character and a heart guided by pure intentions.

> *"First cleanse the inside of the cup and dish, that the outside may also be clean"*
> (Matthew 23:26, NKJV).

Chapter Five

The Heart of Authenticity: Integrity and Sincerity

In today's world, where superficiality and pretense are pervasive, the pursuit of authenticity is rare and precious. Authenticity is grounded in integrity and sincerity, guiding individuals to live by their deepest values and beliefs. At its core, authenticity is about living a life that is true to oneself, in which one's inner values and outward actions are in harmony. That is what defines one's character.

The Jesus Christ's teachings in the Gospel of Matthew, chapter 23, verses 25-27 explore the profound significance of integrity and sincerity in pursuing authenticity. In these verses, Jesus criticizes the Pharisees for their hypocrisy and outward display of righteousness, while inwardly, they are full of greed and excess. He warns against the dangers of focusing solely on outward appearances and neglecting the inner self, which is the antithesis of authenticity.

Integrity and sincerity are two essential qualities that shape one's character and are integral to authenticity. Integrity involves being honest, truthful, and having a solid moral compass, while sincerity is genuine, transparent, and authentic to oneself. Living a life of integrity and sincerity requires a deep commitment to self-awareness, self-reflection, and self-improvement.

Authenticity is rare and precious today, but it is essential to living a fulfilling and meaningful life. Integrity and sincerity are the foundation of authenticity, guiding individuals to live in alignment with their deepest values and beliefs. By pursuing authenticity through integrity and sincerity, individuals can live a life that is true to themselves and, in doing so, find true happiness and fulfillment.

> *"There is a way that appears to be correct,
> but in the end, it leads to death."*
> Proverbs 14:12

Defining Authenticity

Authenticity is a unique and valuable quality beyond an individual's superficial appearance or performance. It emanates from the deepest parts of the human heart and encompasses the genuine expression of one's authentic self. It is the state of being free from pretense, deception, or artificiality and is rooted in integrity and sincerity.

Authenticity is about being true to oneself and embracing one's uniqueness without fear of judgment or rejection. It means having the courage and confidence to express oneself honestly and transparently without hiding behind a facade or pretending to be someone else. It requires consistency between inner convictions and outward actions and honesty and transparency in one's words and deeds.

Authenticity is not about presenting a flawless image or projecting an idealized self-image. On the contrary, it is about embracing the fullness of one's humanity, including vulnerability and imperfection. It is about being comfortable in one's skin and willing to share one's true self without fear of rejection or criticism.

In essence, authenticity is a quality that allows us to connect with others on a deeper level, build trust, and establish meaningful relationships. It is a quality that is highly prized and respected in all areas of life, from personal relationships to business and professional settings.

> *"I have been crucified with Christ, and I no longer live, but Christ lives in me. The life I now live in the body, I live by faith in the Son of God, who loved me and gave himself for me".*
> *Galatians 2:20*

The concept of authenticity is central to the Christian faith. It involves living a life consistent with one's beliefs, particularly the truths in Scripture. In Galatians 2:20, Paul talks about being crucified with Christ so that he no longer lives, but Christ lives in him. This verse highlights the essence of Christian authenticity: living a life that reflects Christ's presence and teachings.

To be authentic, Christians must strive to embody the values and principles of their faith in every aspect of their life. This requires a deep commitment to integrity and sincerity, foundational virtues of a Christian's character and conduct. Authenticity also involves a willingness to be vulnerable and transparent, admit one's shortcomings and failures, and seek forgiveness and grace when needed.

Practically, living an authentic Christian life means being truthful, compassionate, and humble in dealings with others. It means treating others with kindness and respect, even in the face of hostility or opposition. It means being generous with one's time, talents, and resources and using them to serve others and advance the kingdom of God.

Authenticity is a crucial aspect of the Christian faith, which every believer should strive to cultivate in their own life. By reflecting on Christ's presence and teachings, Christians can be powerful witnesses to the world and bring glory to God in all they do.

Biblical Insights

The Bible offers timeless wisdom on the importance of integrity and sincerity in the pursuit of authenticity,

"Whoever walks in integrity walks securely, but whoever takes crooked paths will be found out"
Proverbs 10:9.

The book of Proverbs emphasizes the foundational role of integrity in leading a fulfilling and secure life. It underscores the importance of honesty, sincerity, and moral uprightness in all aspects of life. Individuals who uphold integrity in their thoughts, words, and actions can confidently navigate life with trustworthiness. They are known for their reliability, consistency, and credibility, which earn them the respect and admiration of others.

In contrast, those who engage in deceit and duplicity face severe consequences. They may experience feelings of guilt, shame, and anxiety, which can lead to a breakdown in relationships and a loss of reputation. Their actions can have a ripple effect that extends beyond themselves, impacting their family, friends, and colleagues.

Moreover, their lies may eventually be exposed, further damaging their credibility and trustworthiness.

The book of Proverbs teaches us that integrity is essential to leading a fulfilling and secure life. It is a quality that should be cultivated and upheld in all our lives, from personal relationships to professional endeavors. By staying true to our values and principles, we can confidently navigate life with trustworthiness and earn the respect and admiration of others.

Interpreting the Passage

The book challenges us to reflect on our daily choices and how they impact our lives. It reminds us that integrity is not just a matter of outward behavior but springs from the depths of the heart. Genuine authenticity is rooted in consistently aligning our inner values and beliefs with our outward conduct.

The book further highlights the dangers of dishonesty and deceit. It cautions that attempts to conceal the truth or manipulate others may provide temporary advantages but ultimately lead to disillusionment and loss of trust.

Authenticity, therefore, requires a commitment to honesty and transparency, even when difficult or inconvenient. We must strive to be truthful in all situations, even when it requires admitting our flaws or mistakes.

Living authentically also means being self-aware and examining our beliefs and values to ensure they align with our actions. The book encourages us to practice self-reflection and introspection to better understand ourselves and our motivations. By doing so, we can make better choices that align with our true selves and lead to a more fulfilling life.

The book emphasizes the importance of integrity, honesty, transparency, and aligning our inner values with our behavior. It encourages us to examine our choices, be self-aware, and practice self-reflection to live a more authentic and fulfilling life.

Contemporary Reflections: Relevance Today

In today's world, where social media and digital communication have become ubiquitous, it can be hard to distinguish between reality and perception. This has led to an increased need for authenticity, as many individuals strive to present an idealized image of themselves, often at the expense of their true selves.

Recent research has demonstrated that authenticity is personally fulfilling and crucial for building genuine connections and fostering trust in relationships. People tend to gravitate toward others who are sincere, authentic, and willing to show vulnerability and honesty in their interactions.

Embracing Authenticity

> *"Whoever walks in integrity walks securely."*
> Proverbs 10:9

Strategies for Cultivating Authenticity

The Bible guides how to cultivate authenticity in one's life. Believers need to understand practical strategies that can help them achieve this goal. One such strategy is self-reflection. By examining their values, beliefs, and motivations, believers can gain insight into what matters most. They can then align their actions with their inner convictions, as outlined in the word of God. Regular self-reflection is crucial because it helps enhance self-awareness and strengthen integrity.

Another critical strategy is honest communication. Believers must practice open and sincere communication in their relationships. They must authentically share their thoughts, feelings, and experiences. By doing so, they can encourage others to do the same, creating an environment of trust, honesty, and transparency. Honest communication allows for a deeper understanding of oneself and others, leading to stronger relationships and a greater sense of authenticity.

> *"Authentic dialogue fosters genuine connections and mutual understanding."*

Vulnerability

Vulnerability is a profound characteristic integral to the human experience and spirituality, especially for those who identify as children of God. Recognizing that vulnerability is not a sign of weakness, but rather a fundamental source of inner strength is essential. Embracing vulnerability involves being authentic, open, and sincere, even in moments of discomfort or uncertainty. This willingness to embrace vulnerability is transformative in spiritual relationships, as it lays the groundwork for deepening intimacy and fostering trust with a higher power and fellow believers. As articulated in 2 Corinthians 12:9, embracing vulnerability is paramount for experiencing peace and freedom when we surrender to the divine will.

> **"but he said to me, My grace is sufficient for you, for my power is made perfect in weakness"**
> 2 Corinthians 12:9

Consistency

Consistency is a crucial element for believers to uphold in their daily lives. It involves aligning not only their words and actions but also their thoughts with the values and principles of the Bible, even in the face of challenging circumstances. Consistency is not just about outward behavior; it is about maintaining integrity and demonstrating steadfastness in living out one's faith. When believers consistently act in a manner that reflects their deeply held beliefs, it serves as a powerful testament to their unwavering commitment to their faith. This consistent alignment of belief and behavior builds credibility and trustworthiness, enhancing their authenticity as faith followers.

> *"Whatever you do, work at it with all your heart, as working for the Lord, not for human masters, ²⁴ since you know you will receive an inheritance from the Lord as a reward. It is the Lord Christ you are serving".*
> Colossians 3:23-24

Self-compassion

The practice of self-compassion plays a vital role in the journey towards authenticity. Those on this path must prioritize self-compassion, embrace their imperfections, and understand that authenticity is a continual journey rather than a fixed destination. It is crucial to acknowledge that making mistakes is a natural part of this process. By treating oneself with kindness and understanding while striving to live authentically, individuals are not only better equipped, but also supported and encouraged to navigate life's inevitable challenges with grace and humility.

> *"Therefore, as God's chosen people, holy and clearly loved, clothe yourselves with compassion, kindness, humility, gentleness and patience"*
> Colossians 3:12

Colossians 3:12, the Apostle Paul provides a comprehensive guide to Christian conduct. He emphasizes the development of virtues such as compassion, kindness, humility, gentleness, and patience, essential in nurturing a Christ-like character. These attributes shape individual behavior and play a crucial role in fostering positive and harmonious relationships within Christian communities, strengthening the bonds of our shared faith.

The passage highlights the significance of embodying these virtues as they serve as tangible evidence of God's transformative power in an individual's life. Moreover, this authentic display of faith is a compelling testimony to the profound truths in the Gospel.

Biblical Insights

Matthew 23:25-27

This section is a remarkable combination of theological insight and practical advice, drawing on Bible references to anchor the discussion in scriptural authority. The book of Matthew 23:25-27 is a noteworthy example of how Jesus delivered a poignant rebuke to the religious leaders of the time, the Scribes and Pharisees. In this powerful passage, Jesus condemns their hypocrisy, likening them to whitewashed tombs—beautiful on the outside but filled with decay and uncleanness within.

Jesus begins the rebuke by addressing the outward rituals of purity observed by the scribes and Pharisees. He compares them to cups and dishes meticulously cleansed the outside but

Authentic Spiritual Values

contaminated with greed and self-indulgence within. This metaphor powerfully indicts the hypocrisy that arises when external appearances mask inner corruption.

Continuing his powerful rebuke, Jesus portrays the scribes and Pharisees as whitewashed tombs—ornate and pristine on the outside but concealing death and uncleanness within.

This vivid imagery underscores the danger of prioritizing appearances over authenticity, warning against the spiritual decay that results from such hypocrisy. Jesus calls out the scribes and Pharisees for their lack of authenticity and failure to live up to the high moral standards they were expected to uphold.

Interpreting the Passage

The passage from the Gospel of Matthew in chapter 23, verses 25-27, is a powerful message that provides deep insights into the nature of authenticity and the pitfalls of superficiality. Jesus' teachings urge us to reflect on our hearts' condition and recognize that genuine authenticity must begin from within. It calls us to prioritize inner purity and integrity over outward displays of righteousness, as it is the foundation for proper spiritual growth.

The metaphor of the cup and dish reminds us that authentic spirituality cannot be reduced to mere external observance of religious rituals. It requires a genuine commitment to moral and ethical principles deeply rooted in the human heart. We must cultivate a vibrant inner life characterized by love, compassion, and humility. Genuine authenticity demands

Authentic Spiritual Values

that we live a life consistent with our beliefs and values, both in our private and public lives.

> "May integrity and uprightness protect me because my hope, LORD, is in you." Psalm 25:21

Note: This indicates that integrity is not only a moral attribute but also a form of reliance on God's protection and guidance.

The imagery of the whitewashed tombs serves as a sobering reminder of the dangers of hypocrisy. It warns against the temptation to present a facade of righteousness while harboring moral corruption and deceit. Genuine authenticity requires transparency and honesty, even when it exposes our vulnerabilities and imperfections. Only when we are willing to acknowledge our weaknesses and work towards improving ourselves can we truly grow and become better human beings.

Contemporary Reflections: Relevance Today

Matthew 23:25-27 was initially delivered to a specific audience in a particular historical context, but its message continues to resonate with timeless relevance. In today's fast-paced world, where social media and digital platforms significantly impact our perceptions of self and others, the pressure to maintain appearances can be overwhelming.

Many people find reconciling their inner values and beliefs with external expectations and pressures challenging. Projecting an accurate image of success and happiness can be all-consuming, even if it does not align with one's true self. However, the pursuit of authenticity calls us to embrace vulnerability and honesty, recognizing that true fulfillment comes from living in alignment with our deepest values.

At times, it may be tempting to prioritize external validation over internal truths, especially in the face of societal pressures. However, the pursuit of authenticity requires us to recognize that true happiness and contentment come from living in harmony with our innermost selves. This involves being honest about our strengths and weaknesses, prioritizing our values above external validation, and embracing our unique identities.

Note: he journey toward authenticity is a lifelong process that requires courage, vulnerability, and a willingness to be true to ourselves.

Biblical Understanding of Integrity

(Integrity is often associated with completeness, uprightness, and wholeness)

"The integrity of the upright guides them, but their duplicity destroys the unfaithful." Proverbs 11:3

This verse emphasizes the importance of integrity in one's life, highlighting its significance for personal benefit, guidance, and protection. Living a life of integrity should be a top priority for everyone. One of the most prominent examples of a person with unwavering integrity in the Bible is Job. Even when he faced immense challenges and turmoil, Job remained steadfast in his principles and morals. He is famously known for his statement, reflecting his unshakable commitment to integrity even in adversity.

> *"Till I die, I will not put away my integrity from me"*
> (Job 27:5).

Note: steadfast adherence to righteousness, even in adversity, is a powerful example for believers.

Biblical Understanding of Sincerity

In the Bible, sincerity is not simply about being truthful but is characterized by honesty, genuineness, and the absence of deceit. The apostle Paul emphasizes this in 2 Corinthians 1:12, where he discusses conducting oneself in the world with simplicity and godly sincerity, not by earthly wisdom but by God's grace. This verse highlights sincerity as a reflection of divine influence rather than human cunning. It suggests genuine sincerity comes from humility and dependence on God rather than any personal agenda or desire for personal gain. Therefore, sincerity is not just an outward show of honesty. Still, instead, it reflects one's relationship with God and a willingness to be guided by His wisdom and grace.

> *"Now this is our boast: Our conscience testifies that we have conducted ourselves in the world, especially in our relations with you, with integrity[b]*
> *and godly sincerity*
> *We have done so, relying not on worldly wisdom but on God's grace".*
> 2 Corinthians 1:12

Authentic Spiritual Values

Jesus Christ is known for his teachings that promote sincerity and authenticity in all aspects of life. His teachings emphasize the importance of sincerity in worship and dealings with others. In the book of Matthew, chapter 6, verse 1, Jesus cautions against performing acts of righteousness for the sake of being noticed by people.

He encourages his followers to seek approval from God instead of seeking validation from others. According to Jesus, a pure and sincere heart motivated to please God is more valuable than any human recognition. Therefore, it is essential to cultivate sincerity in our hearts and actions, both in our relationship with God and in our interactions with other people.

> *"Be careful not to practice your righteousness in front of others to be seen by them.*
> *If you do, you will have no reward from your heavenly Father.*
> Matthew. 6:1

Ananias and Sapphira

"Now, Ananias and his wife Sapphira also sold a piece of property. With his wife's full knowledge, he kept back part of the money for himself but brought the rest and put it at the apostles' feet".

Then Peter said, "Ananias, how is it that Satan has so filled your heart that you have lied to the Holy Spirit and have kept for yourself some of the money you received for the land? Didn't it belong to you before it was sold? And after it

Authentic Spiritual Values

was sold, wasn't the money at your disposal? What made you think of doing such a thing? You have not lied just to human beings but to God."

When Ananias heard this, he fell and died. And great fear seized all who heard what had happened. Then, some young men came forward, wrapped up his body, carried him out, and buried him.

About three hours later, his wife came in, not knowing what had happened. Peter asked her, "Tell me, is this the price you and Ananias got for the land?". "Yes," she said, "that is the price."

Peter asked her, "How could you conspire to test the Spirit of the Lord? Listen! The feet of the men who buried your husband are at the door, and they will carry you out also."

At that moment, she fell at his feet and died. Then the young men came in and, finding her dead, carried her out and buried her beside her husband. Great fear seized the whole church and everyone who heard about these events.
Acts 5:1-11

The biblical account of Ananias and Sapphira, as recorded in Acts 5:1-11, is a cautionary tale that highlights the severe consequences of dishonesty and insincerity, especially in the context of religious communities. Ananias and Sapphira sold a piece of property and kept back a portion of the proceeds for themselves, pretending to give the entire amount to the apostles. This deception was a breach of trust and a lie they told the Holy Spirit. As a result, they both fell dead, one after the other, before the apostolic community.

This story underscores the importance of sincerity and authenticity in faith and interactions with others. It shows that God values truthfulness and integrity and that there are severe consequences for those who act deceitfully or hypocritically. The account of Ananias and Sapphira serves as a potent reminder that we should always strive to be honest and genuine in our relationships with God and others.

Living Authentically: Practical Applications

Living with integrity and sincerity is essential to a meaningful and fulfilling life. It means honesty, trustworthiness, and consistency in our actions and decisions, even when no one is watching.

"Whatever you do, work at it with all your heart, as working for the Lord, not for human masters." Colossians 3:23-24

This passage encourages us to apply sincerity and integrity in every aspect of our lives, including work, relationships, and worship. It reminds us that we should always strive to do our best, not for personal gain or recognition, but to honor and glorify God. Therefore, living with integrity and sincerity requires us to be intentional in our thoughts and actions, be true to ourselves and others, and always act honestly and fairly.

Integrity is the quality of being truthful in speech, faithful in commitments, and consistent in character, regardless of

Authentic Spiritual Values

circumstances or audience. A person of integrity is known for their honesty, reliability, and moral principles.

Integrity is emphasized in various religious and ethical traditions, and the Bible is no exception. Daniel's story is an excellent example of integrity. When he was taken as a captive to Babylon, he refused to compromise on his dietary and worship practices, which were by Jewish law and tradition. Despite the pressure from his captors and the temptation to conform to the Babylonian culture, he stood firm on his principles, trusting in God's provision and protection.

This story inspires believers to adhere to their principles even when faced with difficult situations or people who do not share their values. Integrity is not always straightforward, and it often requires sacrifice and courage. However, it is a crucial aspect of the character. that builds trust, respect, and credibility in personal and professional relationships.

> ***"But Daniel resolved not to defile himself with the royal food and wine and asked the chief official for permission not to defile himself this way."***
> Daniel 1:18

Embracing Authenticity

The quality of genuine authenticity is highly regarded, as it encompasses a person's entire character, including integrity, sincerity, and forthrightness in all aspects of their life. This trait requires a deep commitment to aligning one's innermost values with one's outward demeanor, which means consistently taking actions that align with one's beliefs. The biblical reference in Matthew 23:25-27 emphasizes the importance of being true to oneself and encourages us to embrace vulnerability, honesty, and consistency. By living a life of authenticity, one can gain the admiration and trust of those around them. It's important to note that authenticity is not about being perfect but authentic. It's about being open and transparent, even when uncomfortable or difficult.

It's about being honest about our strengths and weaknesses and admitting when we make mistakes. Ultimately, authenticity is about being true to oneself and living a life aligned with one's values, which can lead to greater fulfillment, happiness, and success in all areas of life.

> *"Whoever walks in integrity walks securely."*
> Proverbs 10:9

Living an authentic Christian life is not just about making ethical choices; it requires a more profound commitment to integrity and sincerity. As followers of Christ, we are called to align our actions with biblical teachings and reflect His light in every aspect of our lives. This means we should strive to embody authenticity in everything we do.

Integrity

Integrity is a core value that should guide our daily decisions and interactions. It requires us to be honest, transparent, and accountable, even when no one is watching. Integrity builds trust and credibility and leads to security and fulfillment.

When we have integrity, we can confidently face any challenge and stanfirm in our beliefs.

> *"The righteous man walks in his integrity; his children are blessed after him".*
> Proverbs 20:7

Sincerity

The concept of sincerity encompasses being genuine, honest, and transparent in our words and actions. It means that we are not pretending to be something we are not, and we are not being hypocritical in our interactions with others. When sincere, we prioritize forming authentic connections with others, fostering trust, and nurturing respectful relationships. This sincerity also empowers us to stay firm in our dedication to our principles, even in difficult situations, demonstrating our unwavering commitment to our values. The importance of authenticity in these interactions cannot be overstated, as it makes each individual feel valued and integral to the process.

As we pursue authenticity, we must remember that it is a lifelong journey that requires grace and compassion. We will make mistakes and fall short of our ideals occasionally. However, if we are committed to integrity and sincerity, we can always get back on track and keep moving forward. Ultimately, pursuing authenticity enriches our lives and brings us closer to God.

Chapter Six

Overcoming Hypocrisy: Practical Steps for Spiritual Growth

Overcoming hypocrisy within the church is a challenging but transformative experience that can lead to profound spiritual growth and stronger community ties. When believers start living out their faith authentically, they develop a deeper and more meaningful relationship with God and become part of a more vibrant and supportive faith community.

The church must cultivate a culture of transparency and trust to create an environment of authenticity and honesty. When the church community is free from hypocrisy, genuine relationships among members are strengthened, and these qualities are enhanced. By building stronger bonds of friendship and fellowship among its members, the church can create a more supportive and nurturing community.

> **"The integrity of the upright will guild them".**
> Proverbs 11:3

The bible provides practical steps to help readers navigate the challenges of avoiding hypocrisy and cultivating an authentic relationship with God. To understanding the factors that can lead to hypocrisy in the church is vital to overcoming it. This book explores some ideas from psychological theory to explain how behaviors are formed and how beliefs and behaviors can sometimes clash. By gaining a deeper understanding of these dynamics, readers will be better equipped to avoid hypocrisy, foster a more meaningful relationship with God, and build stronger connections with one another.

> *"Which states, "All the believers were one in heart and mind. No one claimed their possessions were theirs, but they shared everything they had. "*
> Acts 4:32

Psychological Theory

Applying psychological theory to explain how believers can develop and embrace authenticity, we can gain a better understanding of how behaviors are formed and how beliefs and behaviors may intersect or conflict. By examining these dynamics, we can obtain valuable insights into the factors that lead to hypocritical behavior and develop effective strategies to address and prevent such behavior. Equipped with these valuable tools, we can strive to establish a more genuine and supportive faith community where openness, integrity, and confidence are the cornerstones of authentic relationships among members.

The Cognitive dissonance theory

Cognitive dissonance is a well-known psychological concept introduced by Leon Festinger in 1957. The term refers to the mental discomfort that arises when an individual holds two conflicting beliefs, values, or attitudes. The experience of cognitive dissonance is characterized by unease, tension, and confusion, which can be distressing for individuals struggling to reconcile their conflicting thoughts.

Authentic Spiritual Values

In the context of religion, cognitive dissonance can be seen in people's struggles when their behaviors conflict with their spiritual beliefs. For example, in Romans 7:15-25, the Apostle Paul discusses his experience of cognitive dissonance, where his actions contradict his spiritual desires. This is a classic example of cognitive dissonance, where Paul experiences guilt and confusion due to his conflicting thoughts and behaviors.

> ***"For I do not do what I want, but I do the very thing I hate."***
> Romans 7:15

Galatians 5:17 is a book in the New Testament that describes the conflict between the flesh and the spirit, which can be understood as an internal struggle between our carnal desires and our spiritual aspirations. This

Conflict is often characterized by cognitive dissonance, a psychological phenomenon where we experience mental stress or discomfort when we hold two or more contradictory beliefs or values. In the context of Galatians 5:17, the conflict arises from our natural inclination towards sin and our desire to follow the teachings of Jesus Christ. This can create tension as we reconcile worldly desires with spiritual goals.

The passage encourages us to choose the path of righteousness and to allow the Holy Spirit to guide us in our decision-making process. Ultimately, the message of Galatians 5:17 is one of personal growth and spiritual transformation, urging us to strive for a life of virtue and faith.

"For the flesh desires what is contrary to the Spirit, and the Spirit what is contrary to the flesh. They conflict with each other so that you are not to do whatever[c] you want".
Galatians 5:17

Cognitive dissonance is a psychological concept that refers to the discomfort or inner conflict experienced by an individual when their beliefs and actions are inconsistent. It arises when an individual holds two or more contradictory beliefs or values or when their behavior conflicts with their beliefs or values.

The resulting conflict can cause mental stress, anxiety, and a sense of discomfort aligning one's behavior with one's spiritual beliefs is essential to achieving greater inner harmony and reducing cognitive dissonance. This involves being true to oneself and one's values and trying to live by them. For instance, as believers, we uphold the value of honesty but may sometimes engage in deceitful behavior.

This can create a sense of inner conflict and discomfort, which can be resolved by acknowledging the discrepancy and aligning our behavior with our beliefs. Cognitive dissonance is a natural phenomenon that arises when our beliefs and actions are inconsistent. By recognizing the conflict and aligning our behavior with our values, we can achieve greater inner harmony and reduce mental stress and anxiety.

By behaving honestly, they reduce discomfort and improve their well-being.

How to Overcome Cognitive Dissonance

Psychological research suggests that self-awareness and self-regulation are crucial components of personal growth. Self-awareness involves deeply understanding one's thoughts, feelings, and behaviors. By becoming more self-aware, individuals can recognize areas where they need to improve and develop. On the other hand, self-regulation involves learning to manage one's thoughts and behaviors in response to different situations. Practices like journaling, therapy, or mindfulness can help individuals become more aware of their internal processes and develop greater self-control.

In addition to self-awareness and self-regulation, understanding the social factors that influence behavior can help individuals resist the pressure to conform to hypocritical standards. Research has shown that people may feel obligated to adhere to certain societal norms or expectations, even if they conflict with their beliefs and values. By recognizing these social influences, individuals can make conscious behavior choices and act according to their true beliefs and values are to live a fulfilling and authentic life.

When it comes to spiritual practice, adopting the principles of self-awareness and self-regulation can significantly aid believers, including clergy, in living lives more aligned with biblical teachings. Such practices enhance personal spiritual growth and fortify the moral and spiritual health of the entire church community. According to the Bible, church leaders play a crucial role in helping individuals resolve conflicts by encouraging alignment between belief and behavior.

Authentic Spiritual Values

Authenticity in spiritual practice means aligning one's internal beliefs with external actions. By doing so, individuals can establish a deeper connection with their faith while dismantling the facade of hypocrisy and striving for genuine sincerity in their spiritual practice. This includes being honest with oneself and others and living by the scriptures.

> ***"You cannot drink the cup of the Lord and the cup of demons, too; you cannot have a part in both the Lord's table and the table of demons."***
> 1 Corinthians 10:21

Self-reflection and examination are vital tools for personal growth and development. They involve profoundly Introspection is a process of examining one's beliefs, values, and experiences to identify areas of inconsistency. It is a process where an individual looks inward to understand their thoughts, feelings, and behaviors.

Through honest self-reflection, one can identify one's biases, blind spots, and areas of hypocrisy. This allows one to work towards spiritual authenticity, where one's actions align with one's beliefs. For instance, if someone believes in treating others with kindness and respect but often finds themselves being rude or dismissive, self-reflection can help them identify the root cause of this inconsistency and work towards changing their behavior.

Self-reflection and examination can be challenging, as they require a willingness to be honest and vulnerable with oneself. However, they are also advantageous, leading to increased self-awareness, personal growth, and a more fulfilling life.

Authentic Spiritual Values

> ***"Let us examine our ways and test them and let us return to the LORD."***
> Lamentations 3:40

One of the most vital aspects of spiritual growth is introspection. Individuals must ask tough questions and reflecting on their actions, thoughts, and emotions enables believers to better understand themselves and identify areas of their lives where they may be falling short of their spiritual values.

Self-reflection helps individuals identify their strengths and weaknesses and recognize patterns in their behavior that may hinder their spiritual growth. By examining their thoughts and emotions, individuals can understand how they react to different situations and people. This awareness can help them to make better choices in the future and improve their relationships with others.

Moreover, self-reflection can help individuals identify negative beliefs or attitudes and work towards changing them. By doing so, they can align their thoughts and actions with their spiritual beliefs and values, leading to a more fulfilling and purposeful life.

By engaging in regular self-reflection, individuals can gain a deeper understanding of themselves, identify areas of improvement, and take steps toward making positive changes in their lives. This practice is essential for spiritual growth and can help individuals live more fulfilling and meaningful lives.

Authentic Spiritual Values

> *"Search me, God, and know my heart; test me and know my anxious thoughts. See if there is any offensive way in me and lead me in the way everlasting."*
> Psalm 139:23-24

Living according to the scriptures requires one to have a consistent practice of self-evaluation. This means regularly examining one's thoughts and actions to ensure they align with the teachings of the scriptures. Psalm 139:23-24 encourages believers to ask God to search their hearts and minds, to reveal any discrepancies between the person they present to the public and their true self.

When such discrepancies are identified, repentance is necessary. This involves acknowledging one's wrongdoing and asking for forgiveness from God and anyone affected by the action. By doing this, individuals can align their actions with their beliefs and live a life that is in harmony with the teachings of the scriptures.

> *"Let us examine our ways and test them, and let us return to the LORD." This verse emphasizes the need for self-examination as a part of spiritual growth and repentance.*
> Lamentations 3:40

Repentance and Transformation

Repentance and transformation are two vital concepts in Christianity that are often intertwined. Repentance refers to turning away from one's sins and seeking forgiveness from

Authentic Spiritual Values

God. It is a crucial first step towards transformation, which involves completely changing one's beliefs, attitudes, and behavior to align more closely with God's teachings.

Romans 12:2 explains that believers should not conform to the patterns of this world, which are often contrary to God's will. Instead, they should allow the Holy Spirit to renew their minds and transform them to reflect Christ's character. This transformation is a lifelong process that involves learning to love God with all our heart, soul, mind, and strength and to love our neighbors as ourselves.

In essence, repentance and transformation are two sides of the same coin. Repentance is the initial step toward transformation, the ongoing process of aligning our lives with God's will. Through repentance and transformation, we can experience God's forgiveness, grace, and love and become more like Christ in every aspect of our lives.

> *"Do not conform to the pattern of this world but be transformed by the renewing of your mind. Then you will be able to test and approve what God's will is—his good, pleasing, and perfect will".*
> Romans 12:2

The concept of repentance is one of the most fundamental and vital aspects of the Christian faith, deeply rooted in the Greek term "metanoia." This term means a change of mind or a turning around. From a Christian perspective, repentance involves a radical transformation of heart and behavior, moving away from sin and aligning oneself with the will of God.

Repentance is a transformative process that demands individuals to acknowledge their sins, turn away from them, and turn towards God. It's a continuous process that requires personal commitment and dedication to follow the Five Steps of Repentance. This process includes acknowledging the sin, feeling remorse for it, asking for Forgiveness and restitution, and committing to change one's behavior.

The Bible highlights the significance of repentance in many verses, but particularly in Acts 2:38, where Peter says, "Repent and be baptized, every one of you, in the name of Jesus Christ for the forgiveness of your sins, and you will receive the gift of the Holy Spirit." Repentance is not just about feeling guilty or sorry for one's actions; it involves a profound and transformative change of heart, mind, and behavior.

Repentance is a crucial component of the Christian faith as it is linked to salvation. It is a process of turning around and changing one's life, requiring a willingness to admit wrongdoing and seek forgiveness and reconciliation. The transformative power of repentance can lead to a life of joy, peace, and fulfillment, aligned with God's will.

> *"I tell you that in the same way, there will be more rejoicing in heaven over one sinner who repents than ninety-nine righteous persons who do not need to repent."*
> Luke 15:7

Repentance is a crucial process in a Christian's life. It is a continuous process that involves several steps. The first step is recognizing and acknowledging one's sins. This involves identifying specific actions or attitudes that are contrary to biblical standards. It requires a deep understanding of the Word of God and a willingness to examine oneself honestly.

The second step is experiencing genuine sorrow and remorse for one's sins. This sorrow should not be out of fear of punishment but because of the realization that one's actions grieve God. It requires a heart that is sensitive to the leading of the Holy Spirit and a willingness to be broken before God.

The third step is confessing one's sins openly to God. This step requires humility and honesty. It involves acknowledging one's wrongdoing and seeking forgiveness from God. When appropriate, seeking reconciliation with those wronged is also part of this step.

The fourth step is making a deliberate effort to turn away from sin. This step requires action. It may involve seeking help from a mentor or accountability partner setting up accountability measures, or making restitution, require a commitment to change and a willingness to fight against the temptation to sin.

Finally, turning to God and redirecting one's life towards Him. This step involves seeking to live according to God's will through the power of the Holy Spirit. It requires a deepening relationship with God and a willingness to surrender one's life to Him.

The process of repentance is continuous and essential for personal growth and spiritual maturity. As individuals grow in their faith and understanding, they become more aware of the subtleties of sin in their lives and their ongoing need for God's grace. Through the continuous process of repentance, individuals can experience a more profound sense of God's forgiveness and transformation.

> *"Therefore, you Israelites, I will judge each of you according to your ways, declares the Sovereign LORD. Repent! Turn away from all your offenses; then sin will not be your downfall".*
> Ezekiel 18:30

> *"Rid yourselves of all the offenses you have committed and get a new heart and spirit.*
> *Why will you die, people of Israel? ³² For I take no pleasure in the death of anyone, declares the Sovereign LORD. Repent and live!".*
> Ezekiel 18:31-32.

Believers need to hold themselves accountable to overcome hypocrisy. Individuals with solid beliefs must take responsibility for their actions to avoid being hypocritical. One way to achieve this is by being part of a trusted spiritual community, which can provide guidance and support to prevent hypocrisy from taking root in one's life.

Being part of a spiritual community means that individuals are surrounded by people who share similar values and beliefs. This can help hold them accountable for their actions and prevent them from straying from their beliefs. By confessing their faults and seeking guidance from their community, believers can maintain their spiritual integrity and stay true to their beliefs.

Confessing one's faults and seeking guidance is essential to maintaining spiritual integrity. Being honest about one's mistakes and shortcomings can help individuals address them and prevent them from becoming hypocritical. Seeking guidance from a trusted spiritual leader or mentor can provide valuable insights and advice on staying true to one's beliefs.

"Therefore, confess your sins to each other and pray for each other so that you may be healed. The prayer of a righteous person is powerful and effective"
James 5:16.

The Book of James, Chapter 5, Verse 16, is a reminder of the importance of accountability in the spiritual journey. It emphasizes the significance of confessing our sins and praying for each other so that we may be healed. The verse further states that the prayer of a righteous person is powerful and effective. This aspect of accountability is crucial in the journey of faith, as it allows us to have someone who acts as a mirror, reflecting the truth about our lives and helping us stay on the path of righteousness.

An accountability partner provides us with support and encouragement, enabling us to remain true to our beliefs and lead a life of integrity. Through this practice, we benefit from our partners' support and learn to be accountabile for our actions and this is a vital aspect of our spiritual growth.

The accountability practice can be a powerful tool in assisting believers in remaining steadfast in their faith and avoiding temptations that may lead them astray. It provides a safe space for individuals to discuss their struggles, fears, and doubts and receive guidance and support from their partner. Having someone to hold us accountable helps us stay focused on our goals and remain committed to living a life that pleases God.

> ***God is spirit, and his worshipers must worship in the Spirit and truth."***
> John 4:24.

Believers who desire to experience a profound connection with God must align their inner beliefs with their outward actions.

This alignment forms the foundation of a genuine spiritual relationship with God and allows for a more profound experience of His presence, guidance, and peace. Authentic worship and devotion are emphasized in John 4:24 states that God is spirit, and His worshipers must worship in spirit and truth.

Hypocrisy can hinder spiritual growth and weaken community ties within the church. Overcoming hypocrisy requires believers to live out their faith authentically, creating a culture of transparency and trust within the community. This transparency leads to a deeper relationship with God and an enriched faith community.

Authentic Spiritual Values

In thriving church community individuals are encouraged to share their challenges and successes without fear of judgment. This kind of community serves as a model for compassion and empowerment, enabling people to support each other through difficult times and celebrate each other's victories. It is essential to have accountability within this community to prevent hypocrisy and maintain spiritual integrity. Confessing faults and seeking guidance from trusted spiritual partners can help believers stay on the right path.

> ***"Therefore, confess your sins to each other and pray for each other so that you may be healed. The prayer of a righteous person is powerful and effective."***
> James 5:16

The book of James emphases the healing power of confession and prayer in relation to the importance of accountability and having an accountability partner in helping us see the truth about ourselves and stay true to our values. A vibrant, God-centered community is built on openness, trust, and accountability. Believers living authentically create an environment conducive to spiritual growth and development. Such a community can serve as a beacon of hope and love, inspiring others to seek a deeper relationship with God.

(The Church)

Overcoming Hypocrisy: Practical Steps for Spiritual Growth

"If anyone causes one of these little ones—those who believe in me—to stumble, it would be better for them to have a large millstone hung around their neck and to be drowned in the depths of the sea.
⁷ Woe to the world because of the things that cause people to stumble!
Such things must come, but woe to the person through whom they come!".
Matthew 18: 6-7.

Explanations of Key Terms

In Matthew 18:6-7, Jesus warns leaders about the dangers of hypocrisy and highlights the importance of guiding their communities towards genuine spiritual growth. Jesus uses the term "little ones" to refer to those who have faith in Him, including those who are young in their faith and susceptible to being misled. This highlights the significance of leaders recognizing their influence and the vulnerability of their followers.

Jesus's use of extreme language, such as the image of being drowned with a millstone around the neck, emphasizes the severity of the spiritual consequences of leading others astray.

This underscores the accountability that leaders hold and the need for them to be responsible for their actions.

The Greek word "scandalize" suggests that leaders who lead others into sin or cause them to lose faith through hypocrisy or moral failings are causing them to stumble. Therefore, leaders must align their actions and teachings with Christ's teachings to avoid being a stumbling block.

Verse 7 acknowledges that stumbling blocks are inevitable in a sinful world. However, leaders must still take responsibility for promoting righteousness and not contributing to sin. The pronouncement of "woe" serves as both a lament and a warning of impending judgment. This emphasizes the need for leaders to maintain personal integrity and vigilance as they face divine judgment if they lead others into sin.

The Role of Church Leaders:

Conducting a thorough evaluation of the church in modern times, one cannot help but question the current state of the body of Christ. While it is true that the number of Church has been on the rise, it seems that some individuals are using the church for their gain. This raises concerns about the true intentions of those in positions of power and influence.

As Jesus predicted in the book of Matthew, the church has become a den of robbers. This is evident in the exploitation and manipulation of church members, the mismanagement of funds, and the lack of transparency in decision-making. Instead of being a sanctuary for believers, the church has become a place where some people take advantage of others.

Authentic Spiritual Values

These issues have caused great distress among the faithful, leading to a loss of trust in the church as an institution. However, it is crucial that the church leadership addresses these problems and takes decisive steps to restore the church's credibility and integrity. This potential for change can inspire hope and rekindle faith in the church.

The mission of the church is to serve as a beacon of hope and salvation for believers.

> **"It is written," he said to them, "'My house will be called a house of prayer,'[e] but you are making it's a den of robbers"**
> Matthew 21:13

The present era is marked by a decline in the moral values that have long been associated with the Church. The focus of sermons has shifted towards material gain and the pursuit of worldly pleasures, with leaders often using scriptures to manipulate and deceive people for financial gain. In this time, the size of the cathedral and the grandeur of its crown have become the metrics used to measure the level of salvation, anointing, and the presence of God. However, in this context, we must be reminded of the true essence of faith and called back to God.

This book serves as a vital reminder of the importance of spiritual values and the need to re-center our lives on God.

> **"Enter through the narrow gate. Wide is the gate, and broad is the road that leads to destruction, and many**

enter through it. ¹⁴ But small is the gate and narrow the road that leads to life, and only a few find it.
"Matthew 7:13-14.

People often turn to their religious leaders for guidance and support in conflict. Church leaders are seen as experienced and knowledgeable individuals who can provide valuable counsel, teaching, and assistance to help individuals resolve their problems and align their actions with their faith.

The role of church leaders in resolving conflicts is multifaceted. First and foremost, they are responsible for watching over the souls of their flock and guiding them along the right path. This duty includes providing spiritual support, offering advice, and helping individuals to overcome difficulties beyond their spiritual responsibilities.

Church leaders are also accountable to God for the well-being of their congregation. This underscores the importance of their role in helping individuals navigate dissonance and conflict. By offering guidance and support, leaders can help individuals identify the root causes of their problems, develop coping strategies, and find solutions consistent with their religious beliefs. Church leaders are crucial in helping individuals navigate conflicts and resolve dissonance. Their experience, knowledge and spiritual guidance are invaluable resources for finding peace and harmony.

Have confidence in your leaders and submit to their authority because they watch you as those who must

Authentic Spiritual Values

> ***give an account. Do this so their work will be a joy, not a burden, for that would not benefit you.***
> Hebrews 13:17:

The church is now an investment where investors can buy shares and create generational wealth. The true believers begin to wonder where the church is. Overcoming hypocrisy and promoting spiritual growth within a church community are essential tasks for church leaders.

These goals require a commitment to personal integrity and the development of an authentic faith community. The Bible and psychological principles offer valuable insights into how leaders can effectively nurture spiritual growth and reduce hypocrisy.

> **"Watch out for false prophets. They come to you in sheep's clothing, but inwardly, they are ferocious wolves. By their fruit, you will recognize them. Do people pick grapes from thorn bushes? or figs from thistles? Likewise, every good tree bears good fruit, but a wrong tree bears bad fruit.**
> Matthew 7:15-17.

The Characteristics of the Church Leader

Authentic Spiritual Values

The biblical text of 1 Timothy 4:12 contains a timeless message and is highly relevant to the modern world. It speaks of the importance of authentic leadership characterized by exemplary behavior. The text urges leaders to set an example in their speech, conduct, love, faith, and purity so that they can shape their community.

The transformative power of authentic leadership is highlighted in the text. Leaders who cultivate self-assurance, display exemplary conduct, and foster emotional and spiritual growth can profoundly impact those around them. They are pivotal in shaping the community, and their actions and attitudes directly influence the congregation.

The passage emphasizes the need for leaders to reject negative assessments and promote a positive self-image, by doing so, they can empower the entire community to grow and change. Ultimately, the text's message is clear: authentic leadership is essential for the well-being and growth of any community, and it remains as relevant today as it was when it was first written.

> ***Don't let anyone look down on you because you are young, but set an example for the believers in speech, conduct, love, faith, and purity.***
> 1 Timothy 4:12

Verse 1 Timothy 4:12 powerfully reminds us of the significant impact that a leader's behavior has on the faith and conduct of others. The Apostles recognized it is essential to set an example in various areas to enhance leadership abilities and promote growth in the community.

The Apostles emphasized the need for leaders to cultivate emotional and spiritual maturity, for their well-being and also plays a crucial role in effective relational leadership.

Moreover, church leaders are encouraged to handle criticism maturely and maintain a positive self-image when faced with negativity. This helps to foster a supportive environment that promotes growth and resilience. As a result, leaders can play a pivotal role in shaping the community's values and beliefs and have a transformative impact on their followers.

The timeless advice of Paul to Timothy, which encourages him to set an example in speech, conduct, love, faith, and purity, still holds relevance in today's world. It highlights the enduring importance of authentic leadership, which remains significant even today. Leaders who embody these virtues can inspire their followers and foster a sense of purpose and meaning.

Verse 1 Timothy 4:12 underscores the critical role of leaders in shaping the community's values and beliefs, this highlights the transformative power of leaders who cultivate self-assurance, display exemplary conduct, and foster emotional and spiritual growth.

It emphasizes the need for leaders to reject negative assessments and promote a positive self-image, as their actions and attitudes directly influence the congregation and empower the entire community to grow and change.

Emotional Spiritual Development

Influential leaders must develop emotional and spiritual maturity to ensure personal well-being and relational effectiveness. Emotional maturity allows them to manage emotions and handle situations with composure, while spiritual maturity provides a deeper understanding of oneself and purpose. Cultivating both enables church leaders to lead with wisdom and empathy.

Moreover, Leaders are encouraged to handle criticism maturely by responding constructively and objectively rather than with defensiveness or hostility; this will help them learn from feedback and improve their leadership skills. It is also crucial for Leaders to maintain a positive self-image when faced with negativity, as it can affect their self-esteem, confidence, and mental health.

However, the real power lies in a supportive environment that encourages growth and resilience. This environment inspires and motivates leaders to build a solid and effective team, overcome challenges, and achieve success.

1Timothy 4:12 offers invaluable guidance and a comprehensive roadmap for leaders who aspire to become influential and respected in their communities. It emphasizes the importance of developing essential skills and qualities that enable leaders to positively influence their surroundings and make a meaningful difference in the lives of others. According to the passage.

Authentic Spiritual Values

Leaders must focus on developing self-Perception, understanding their strengths, weaknesses, and values while, using this knowledge to guide their decisions and actions. They must also cultivate role-modeling skills, which include setting a positive example for others and inspiring them to follow suit. Additionally, leaders must strive for emotional and spiritual maturity, which involves developing empathy, compassion, and wisdom and maintaining a solid connection with their faith.

This reiteration of guidance is meant to inspire and motivate leaders on their leadership journey and encourage them to use their talents and skills to impact their communities positively.

The Bible is a rich source of guidance and wisdom for individuals in all walks of life, including leaders. One verse that provides constructive guidance for leaders is 1 Timothy 4:12. This verse encourages leaders to focus on developing key attributes that can help them become more influential and respected in their communities.

1 Timothy 4:12 emphasizes the importance of self-perception. Leaders who can accurately assess their strengths and weaknesses are better equipped to make sound decisions and effectively lead their teams. Additionally, by recognizing their limitations, leaders can work to improve themselves and become better role models for their followers.

Role Modeling

Authentic Spiritual Values

Speaking of role modeling, 1 Timothy 4:12 also stresses the importance of this skill for leaders. Leaders who can lead by example and demonstrate the behaviors they expect from their followers are more likely to earn their respect and trust.

By modeling positive behaviors and attitudes, leaders can create a culture of excellence and inspire their teams to do their best work.

1 Timothy 4:12 encourages leaders to focus on developing their emotional and spiritual maturity. Leaders who can regulate their emotions, stay calm under pressure, and maintain a positive outlook are better equipped to handle leadership challenges. Additionally, by nurturing their spiritual lives and staying connected to a higher purpose, leaders can find meaning and fulfillment in their work, inspiring them to lead with passion and purpose.

1 Timothy 4:12 provides a roadmap for leaders who aspire to become influential and respected. By focusing on developing self-perception, role-modeling skills, and emotional and spiritual maturity, leaders can positively impact their communities and make a meaningful difference.

This 'meaningful difference' can be understood as a positive change that benefits the community, such as fostering unity, promoting justice, or inspiring others to lead with integrity.

This reiteration of guidance is not just a reminder but a testament to the relevance of the book of 1 Timothy in the leadership journey. It provides invaluable support for leaders who aspire to become influential and respected in their communities. Specifically, chapter 4, verse 12 suggests that leaders can achieve this by focusing on three key areas: self-perception, role-modeling skills, and emotional and spiritual maturity.

Self-perception involves clearly understanding one's strengths and weaknesses and cultivating healthy self-esteem and confidence. By doing so, leaders can project a positive image and inspire others to follow their example.

Role-modeling skills refer to the ability to lead by example and set a positive tone for others to follow. This involves demonstrating the values and behaviors one wishes to see in others and consistency in one's actions and words.

Emotional and spiritual maturity are essential for leaders who seek to make a meaningful difference in their communities. This involves developing a deep empathy for others and a solid connection to spiritual beliefs and values, leaders can inspire others to follow their example and create a positive impact in the world.

The Fruits of the Spirit - Galatians **5:22-23**

Galatians 5:22-23 is a prominent scripture passage in Christian spirituality, especially when discussing leadership and personal growth. It emphasizes the importance of cultivating the fruits of the Spirit in one's life to demonstrate spiritual maturity. The fruits of the Spirit are a combination of essential qualities that should be evident in every believer's life, particularly those who lead others. Leaders who aspire to enhance their spiritual health and promote personal growth

Authentic Spiritual Values

can benefit significantly by applying and practicing the qualities listed in Galatians 5:22-23, also known as the "fruit of the Spirit."

The fruits of the Spirit include love, joy, peace, forbearance, kindness, goodness, faithfulness, gentleness, and self-control. These virtues are not just characteristics that one can "put on" externally; they are the natural outflow of a life led by the Holy Spirit. Love is more than just a feeling or emotion; it is a choice to value and serve others. Joy is not dependent on our circumstances; it is a deep sense of contentment from within. Peace is not just.

The absence of conflict, but rather, it is a state of inner calm that transcends situations. Forbearance is the ability to endure difficult circumstances or people patiently.

Kindness is a gentle and compassionate attitude towards others. Goodness is moral uprightness and integrity. Faithfulness is a steadfast commitment to one's beliefs and promises. Gentleness is a meek and humble spirit. Self-Control is exercising restraint over one's thoughts, feelings, and actions.

Nurturing these fruits of the Spirit in their daily lives, leaders can create an environment that promotes personal growth, emotional health, and spiritual maturity in themselves and those they lead and experience personal benefits that enrich their lives and leadership.

Authentic Spiritual Values

> ***"But the fruit of the Spirit is love, joy, peace, forbearance, kindness, goodness, faithfulness, gentleness, and self-control. Against such things there is no law".***
> Galatians 5:22-23

Leaders who aspire to be authentic to their proclaimed beliefs can cultivate virtues that help them avoid hypocrisy. These virtues include honesty, integrity, humility, compassion, and self-awareness.

Consistently, Leaders can practice these virtues to ensure that their actions align with their words and positively impact the people they lead. Leaders can take practical steps to cultivate these virtues.

One of the most important is engaging in spirituality practices such as prayer and meditation on Scripture help leaders stay connected to their faith and develop a deeper understanding of their values and beliefs.

Another helpful practice is regularly reflecting on one's life and identifying areas for growth. This can be done through journaling, self-reflection, or seeking feedback from others. Identifying areas for improvement will help leaders to focus their efforts on developing the virtues they need to be authentic and effective leaders.

Establishing accountability structures can also be helpful. Leaders can find accountability partners or mentors who can help them stay on track and provide guidance and support as they strive to cultivate these virtues. It is also important to model and mentor these virtues. Leaders who exhibit these qualities can inspire and encourage others to do the same. Setting a positive example and providing guidance and support others, leaders can foster a culture of authenticity and growth within their organizations.

Engaging in the community is also essential. Leaders connected to a community of like-minded individuals can draw strength and support from that community and offer support and encouragement to others.

Pursuing ongoing education on spiritual and ethical matters is essential. The world is constantly changing, and leaders need to stay up to date on the latest developments in teaching and mentoring. Since leaders were teachers according to scripture, Leaders who understand their cultural setting will know how to teach others in that environment. By continuing to learn and grow, leaders can stay true to their values and beliefs and be influential leaders who positively impact their communities.

Development of Virtues

*"For this very reason, make every effort to add to your faith goodness; and to goodness, knowledge; **Six** and to knowledge, self-control; self-control, perseverance; and to perseverance, godliness; [7] and to godliness, mutual affection; and mutual affection, love. For if you possess these qualities in increasing measure, they will keep you from being ineffective and unproductive in your knowledge of our Lord Jesus Christ".*
2 Peter 1:5-8 (NIV)

Authentic Spiritual Values

Continuous growth and progressive development are essential to become effective and productive in one's spiritual life. The text highlights that intentionally and continuously developing each quality can prevent stagnation in one's faith.

In addition to highlighting the importance of growth and development, the text provides practical steps for leaders to incorporate these virtues into their lives. It reiterates the importance of leaders' commitment to their own growth and development, emphasizing that by setting specific goals and focusing on educational growth through the study of Scriptures, theological works, and other spiritual writings, leaders can deepen their understanding and application of these teachings. Leaders who draw insights from the social and economic settings of the scripture writers will find it easier to relate bible teaching to current social and economic settings, further enriching their understanding and application of these teachings.

Moreover, the text recommends engaging with a mentor or a peer group for accountability in personal growth. Having someone to guide and support you in the journey of spiritual growth can be beneficial. The text further emphasizes the need for regular reflection and meditation on each virtue and assessing personal growth and areas needing attention.

The text is a comprehensive guide providing practical and actionable steps for Christians to develop virtues and grow spiritually. It emphasizes the importance of continuous growth, development, and accountability in personal growth. Furthermore, it highlights the crucial role of leaders in practicing these virtues within the community. It suggests that leaders must actively demonstrate godliness and mutual affection through service and fostering a nurturing environment within the church or organization. The text encourages leaders to mentor younger believers or less mature leaders in developing these qualities, using personal experiences and insights as teaching tools.

The text highlights that maintaining a positive, faith-driven approach to overcoming obstacles is paramount. It implies that every challenge, difficulty, or trial one encounters should be viewed as an opportunity to practice perseverance and rely more deeply on God. Such an approach can significantly benefit a person's spiritual growth and development, especially when incorporating these virtues into daily life. A leader who practices this approach can foster a genuine and vibrant spiritual life that positively influences others and glorifies God. By Constantly putting faith into action can build a strong foundation for oneself and inspire others to do the same. It is important to remember that every obstacle presents an opportunity to grow and become a better version of oneself.

The structure and purpose of leadership.

"So, Christ himself gave the apostles, the prophets, the evangelists, the pastors, and teachers,
[12] to equip his people for works of service so that the body of Christ may be built up.
[13] until we all reach unity in the faith and the knowledge of the Son of God and become mature, attaining to the whole measure of the fullness of Christ".
Ephesians 4:11-13

Ephesians 4:11-13 offers valuable insights to church leaders on how to guide their congregation towards spiritual growth and maturity. According to the passage, Christ has appointed specific individuals to serve as apostles, prophets, evangelists, pastors, and teachers responsible for equipping the church members to do ministry work. By fulfilling their respective roles and working together in unity, these leaders can foster an environment of love, respect, and mutual support. This is not just a suggestion, but a responsibility that empowers leaders to create a nurturing environment. As a result, the church can mature in its faith, deepen its understanding of God's word, and reflect Christ's values daily.

Diversity of Leadership Roles (Verse 11)

The church comprises individuals with varying roles and functions, Apostles, Prophets, Evangelists, Pastors, and Teachers. Each role has unique responsibilities and duties essential to the church's overall functioning.

The Apostles

The role of the Apostles is to establish churches and doctrines, serving as the church's foundation. They organize new churches and ensure they adhere to Christ's teachings. Additionally, they are responsible for establishing the doctrines that guide the church's beliefs and practices.

The apostles, as the main conduits of Jesus' teachings, played a pivotal role in establishing the early Christian church. Their writings in the New Testament not only defined authentic spiritual principles but also set doctrinal standards and provided moral guidance. They were instrumental in addressing doctrinal disputes and ethical dilemmas, setting church doctrine, and exemplifying Christian virtues.

As an apostle, Paul's significant contributions to the spread of the Gospel, the establishment of churches, and the provision of rich theological and ethical teachings through his letters cannot be overstated.

Apostle Paul's profound influence as a mentor and leader, particularly in his guidance of leaders such as Timothy and Titus. His teachings on theological truths and the qualities of church leaders continue to resonate and serve as a guide for future generations. Moreover, the text underscores Paul's adept handling of controversies in various communities, highlighting his efforts to uphold the core values of the Gospel while addressing moral failings and doctrinal inaccuracies.

The Prophets

The Prophets bring divine revelation and correction to the church. Their role is to receive and share messages from God that provide guidance and direction to the church. They are also responsible for correcting errors or deviations within the church's teachings or practices.

The role of prophets involves foretelling future events and forth-telling messages of correction, encouragement, or revelation of God's will. For instance, a prophet might forth-tell a message of correction by addressing a specific sin within the church community, or they might forth-tell a message of encouragement by reassuring the believers of God's love and faithfulness. The New Testament acknowledges the role of prophets within the church as one of the spiritual gifts. Agabus, a New Testament prophet, accurately predicted a severe famine, guiding the church to prepare for the crisis, and foretold the fate of Paul, demonstrating the impactful role of a prophet in guiding the church through future challenges.

Prophets correct and challenge the church by confronting ungodly behaviors and calling for repentance. Prophets, through their divine connection, unveil profound spiritual truths, enriching the believers' understanding of the divine plan. Prophets, in times of adversity, serve as beacons of hope, encouraging perseverance and faith by reminding believers of God's unwavering promises and faithfulness. Prophets guide decision-making by revealing God's guidance on specific issues, helping church leaders and members make informed decisions aligned with God's will.

The Evangelists

The Evangelists are responsible for spreading the gospel to those who have not heard it. They share the good news of Christ's life and teachings with the world, bringing new believers into the church.

proclaiming the Gospel, fostering the church's growth, and nurturing believers' faith. Moreover, it emphasizes the Gospel's transformative power in instilling genuine spiritual values and cultivating hope and faith. The text also elaborates on the role of evangelists in guiding spiritual transformation, teaching new converts, and igniting renewal within the church. It emphasizes their function as living examples, motivators for change, and catalysts for spiritual revival. Ultimately, the text aims to inspire our audience to actively engage in spiritual revival by highlighting these pivotal roles.

Pastors and Teachers

The roles of pastors and teachers in the Christian church are crucial as they guide, nurture, and educate the congregation. Their primary responsibility is to equip church members, promoting maturity, unity, and faithfulness within the community, as outlined in Ephesians 4:11-12. The Apostle Paul serves as an exemplary model of both a pastor and a teacher, demonstrating pastoral care and a dedication to teaching through his epistles to various churches. This text underscores the essential responsibilities of pastors and teachers in upholding and communicating biblical truths, exemplifying Christ-like behavior, providing pastoral care, encouraging spiritual disciplines, and fostering community and unity within their congregations.

The inclusion of diverse roles within the church is not just a matter of choice, but a necessity. It prevents any individual or group from accumulating excessive power, which could lead to hypocrisy and corruption. Without this diversity, the church may struggle to maintain a harmonious alignment with the teachings of Christ. This diversity fosters a rich tapestry of perspectives and experiences, enabling the church to effectively fulfill its mission of spreading the gospel and nurturing a deeper connection between individuals and God.

Equipping the Saints (Verse 12)

The statement "To Equip the Saints for the Work of Ministry" refers to a leadership approach emphasizing the importance of training and empowering every believer to minister according to their unique gifts and abilities. This approach aims to prevent leader-centric models that can result in hypocrisy if leaders are perceived as the church community's sole bearers of authority or holiness.

The second statement, "For Building Up the Body of Christ," emphasizes the goal of church leadership: fostering a sense of unity and community within the body of Christ. To achieve this goal, leaders must model integrity and dedication, which are essential for building trust and authenticity within the church. When leaders prioritize building up the church community over individual power or authority, they create a supportive and welcoming environment where believers can thrive and grow in their faith.

Goals of Leadership (Verse 13)

Spiritual leaders are responsible for promoting unity among their followers by emphasizing the shared truth of faith and knowledge of Christ. To counteract hypocrisy, they focus on fostering a communal understanding of faith and knowledge instead of individual Prominence. This approach is essential to the spiritual journey of the community.

Spiritual maturity is a crucial aspect of combating hypocrisy. Mature believers reflect the character of Christ and live out their faith genuinely and consistently. The measure of spiritual

Authentic Spiritual Values

maturity is the fullness of Christ's stature, and all believers should prioritize striving toward this goal.

Leaders must frequently examine their motives and actions to align with Christ's teachings. They should also implement transparent decision-making processes and be accountable to other leaders and members to maintain integrity within their organizations.

Empowering their team can create a culture of service and authenticity. Influential leaders prioritize the team's empowerment and enhance the community's spiritual growth.

Church leaders are responsible for promoting unity and understanding among the congregation. One way to achieve this is by encouraging excellent knowledge and communal worship practices that deepen followers' understanding of faith and Christ's teachings. When church leaders prioritize teaching and preaching grounded

The Bible promotes love, kindness, and compassion, which can help unify the church and reduce divisive behavior. By fostering a sense of community and encouraging open dialogue and discussion, church leaders can create an environment welcoming and supportive of everyone, regardless of their background or beliefs. Promoting unity and understanding is crucial for building a solid, vibrant church community centered around Christ's teachings.

Developing influential leaders requires a focus on character growth, which is more important than mere charisma. Prioritizing character development over surface-level qualities like charm or confidence is essential. This approach ensures that leaders are guided by strong moral principles and are committed to personal growth.

When prioritizing character development, leaders must cultivate spiritual maturity, emotional intelligence, and ethical decision-making. They are compelled to lead by example and model the behaviors they expect from their followers. This creates a culture of trust and respect, which is essential for building strong and effective teams.

In essence, character growth is about developing individuals who are not just competent but also compassionate, empathetic, and morally grounded. It is about cultivating leaders who inspire others to be their best selves and can navigate complex challenges with wisdom and integrity. We can create a more just, equitable, and harmonious world by prioritizing character development.

The Role of the Community

> *"And let us consider how we may spur one another on toward love and good deeds,*
> *²⁵ not giving up meeting together, as some are in the habit of doing, but encouraging one another-and all the more as you see the Day approaching".*
> Hebrews 10;24-25

The book of Hebrews is a crucial text for understanding the importance of community and mutual encouragement in the context of Christian faith. In particular, the book highlights the role of these principles in fostering spiritual growth and combating the dangers of hypocrisy, particularly among

Authentic Spiritual Values

leaders. By embracing the values of community and mutual support, Christian leaders can build a more authentic and active faith community characterized by love, good work, and accountability.

The book of Hebrews emphasizes that community and mutual encouragement are essential for helping Christian leaders address and overcome hypocrisy. Chapter 10, for instance, stresses the importance of proactive engagement among believers to encourage one another to love and do good deeds.

This chapter also highlights the necessity of regular communal interactions to strengthen faith and promote accountability. In this way, the book of Hebrews offers a powerful vision for how Christian leaders can build a solid and supportive faith community. By fostering a mutual encouragement and accountability culture, leaders can help create an environment where believers can flourish and grow in their faith. Ultimately, this can combat the pitfalls of hypocrisy, promote spiritual growth, and build a more authentic and vibrant faith community.

Encouraging One Another (Verse 24)

The text emphasizes motivating each other to love and do good. The act of motivating should be purposeful, energetic, and inspiring. As a leader, one must actively encourage oneself and the community to show love through tangible deeds. This proactive approach helps to combat hypocrisy by prioritizing genuine faith in action. Leaders must adopt a mindful and intentional mindset while pondering motivating their congregation. They must think critically and strategically, considering individual and collective needs and strengths. By doing this, they can create a supportive environment that fosters growth and inspires people to do good.

Consistency (Verse 25)

Consistency is crucial to any gathering, particularly in maintaining spiritual well-being and promoting community cohesion. Regular meetings help leaders stay accountable and ensure their actions align with their words, preventing hypocrisy. Neglecting to meet can create a sense of isolation, which can lead to inconsistency and hypocrisy in spiritual practices. Therefore, leaders must model a steadfast commitment to the community as a fundamental aspect of spiritual growth. By prioritizing the community and showing up consistently, leaders can help cultivate a sense of belonging and foster a strong sense of shared purpose among group members. Ultimately, this can lead to deeper spiritual connections and greater fulfillment.

Encouragement is critical in preventing feelings of isolation and self-centeredness, which can lead to hypocrisy. Leaders must take up the mantle of being sources of encouragement and open to receiving it themselves.

The mention of the impending "Day" (often interpreted as the Day of the Lord or the return of Christ) only amplifies the importance of encouragement. This eschatological viewpoint highlights the significance of living authentically and urgently, with a keen awareness of our future accountability.

The "Day" serves as a reminder that our actions have consequences, and we will be answerable for them. Therefore, living an authentic life that conforms to our values and beliefs is essential while inspiring those around us to do the same. Leaders can create a culture of encouragement by acknowledging the efforts of others, providing constructive feedback, and motivating them to achieve their goals. By doing so, they can help build a supportive, empathetic, and compassionate community and make the world a better place.

Community engagement is an essential aspect of effective leadership. Leaders who prioritize participating in and facilitating regular and meaningful interactions with the community are better able to build trust, establish open lines of communication, and promote transparency and accountability.

Engaging with the community regularly, leaders can gain valuable insights into community needs, concerns, and priorities and use this information to inform decision-making and policy development. Moreover, regular community engagement can help leaders identify and address potential issues before they become significant problems and foster a sense of shared responsibility and collaboration between leaders and their communities. Therefore, leaders must prioritize community engagement and ensure it is an ongoing and meaningful part of their leadership approach.

Community engagement is an essential aspect of effective leadership. Leaders who prioritize participating in and facilitating regular and meaningful interactions with the community are better able to build trust, establish open lines of communication, and promote transparency and accountability. By engaging with the community regularly, leaders can gain valuable insights into community needs, concerns, and priorities and use this information to inform decision-making and policy development. Moreover, regular community engagement can help leaders identify and address potential issues before they become significant problems and foster a sense of shared responsibility and collaboration between leaders and the community they serve.

Therefore, leaders must prioritize community engagement and ensure it is an ongoing and meaningful part of their leadership approach.

Modeling Consistency:

Leaders' involvement in community events and activities is of utmost importance. It not only demonstrates their unwavering commitment to Christ's teachings but also underscores the importance of community service and aiding others. Consistency in attendance and engagement is not just important, it's crucial. It signifies that leaders value the community's welfare and actively strive to make a positive impact. Moreover, it fosters trust and credibility, two vital qualities for effective leadership. Hence, leaders should prioritize their involvement in community events and activities and inspire others to do the same. By leading by example, they can motivate others to follow in their footsteps, thereby fostering a culture of service and commitment to Christ's teachings.

Building an Encouraging Environment

Creating a positive and uplifting atmosphere requires establishing an encouraging environment. This entails fostering a setting where everyone, including leaders, feels supported and motivated. The leaders' encouragement creates a sense of inclusiveness and promotes unity. Individuals can thrive and reach their full potential by cultivating such an environment.

Eschatological Awareness

Christian eschatology, a field of study that focuses on the end of times and the final destiny of humanity, is not a topic to be taken lightly. It is crucial to maintain an awareness of this subject as it can stir us to practice our faith with principle, sincerity, and urgency. Eschatology underscores the transient nature of our current lives and the importance of being prepared for the Day of the Lord, the final judgment day when God will evaluate every person according to their deeds. This awareness should prompt us to prioritize our actions, align them with our values and beliefs, and prepare diligently for the goal of salvation.

Accountability and Boldness

> **"Don't let anyone look down on you because you are young, but set an example for the believers in speech, conduct, love, faith, and purity."**
> 1Timothy 12:4

Authentic Spiritual Values

The books of Timothy and James contain valuable insights on effective leadership within the church. One of the most significant issues these books address is the problem of hypocrisy among church leaders. To combat this problem, the authors suggest two fundamental principles that leaders must follow. These principles revolve around integrity, transparency, and community building.

Timothy teaches the importance of maintaining personal integrity as a leader, which means that leaders must not only talk about their values and beliefs but also live them out in their daily lives. The passage emphasizes the need for leaders to be exemplary in all aspects of their lives and to embody the virtues they preach. By doing so, they can inspire their followers to do the same and create a spiritually mature and responsible community.

Moreover, Timothy encourages leaders to be transparent and open with their followers by being honest about their flaws and mistakes, as well as their successes and achievements; doing so will foster a sense of trust and authenticity within the community. Leaders must also promote transparency in decision-making processes, finances, and other aspects of church governance. Through openness, leaders can build an accountable and responsible community.

The book of James highlights the importance of community building as a key leadership principle. This principle underscores the need for leaders to prioritize the needs of their followers and actively work towards creating an inclusive and welcoming environment. Such an environment fosters a sense of community, where individuals feel valued and supported.

This, in turn, inspires the congregation to grow spiritually and assume responsibility, thereby combating hypocrisy and fostering a spiritually mature and accountable community.

Virtues of Leaders

Model Behavior

Maintaining consistency between your words, beliefs, and actions is essential. You should always ensure that your actions align with the values and principles you publicly profess to follow. You are avoiding any conduct or behavior that contradicts your statements of faith, which can lead to questions about your integrity and credibility. Therefore, being mindful of your actions and how others might perceive them is essential, particularly if you have a public or leadership role. By demonstrating consistency between your beliefs and actions, you can build trust and respect among those around you and establish a strong reputation as a person of integrity.

Authentic Love

Authentic love is a powerful emotion that goes beyond mere words. It involves demonstrating genuine concern and empathy for others. When you truly love someone, you are willing to put their needs above your own and show them compassion and understanding.
This kind of love requires a deep connection with the other person and a willingness to listen to and understand their perspective. It involves being there for them during difficult times, offering a shoulder to cry on and a listening ear.

Authentic love is about building a relationship based on mutual trust and respect and supporting each other through thick and thin.

Spiritual Strength

Developing spiritual strength is a journey that requires a meaningful and sincere connection with God. This can be achieved by engaging in practices such as praying, reading and studying religious texts, attending worship services, and participating in spiritual practices that resonate with you. These practices will help you tap into a deep wellspring of faith and inspiration, guiding you toward a life of resilience and grace. This inner strength will empower you to navigate life's challenges with confidence, living according to your highest principles and values.

Spiritual strength is a set of actions and a profound transformation of who you are. It's about cultivating a sense of purpose and meaning and aligning with your deepest convictions.

By staying connected to God and seeking to live a life of service and compassion, you can embark on a journey of personal growth and develop the spiritual strength you need to thrive in all areas of your life.

Unshakable Faith

Losing sight of what we believe in can be accessible in difficult times; that is why we should have unshakable faith and remember the word of God, especially when faced with opposition or adversity.

> **The LORD himself goes before you and will be with you; he will never leave or forsake you.
> Do not be afraid; do not be discouraged.**
> Deuteronomy 31:8

It's natural to question ourselves and our convictions in the face of challenges; however, holding onto the cross can give us the strength and conviction to overcome any obstacle. Whether it's our values or faith, remembering what we stand for can help us focus on what's truly important. So, let us always remember our beliefs and hold on to them tightly, for they can be a source of inspiration and hope in difficult times.

Integrity in Every Aspect

Maintain integrity in every aspect of our lives, whether in the church, public, or private settings, by always aiming to conduct ourselves ethically and morally and avoiding engaging in any behavior that could compromise our principles or values. Upholding integrity involves honesty, fairness, and transparency in our dealings with others and treating everyone with respect and dignity. It also means being accountable for our actions and mistakes or wrongdoings. Prioritizing integrity in all areas of life, we can build trust, credibility, and a strong sense of character to serve us well in our personal and professional relationships and build the CHURCH OF GOD.

Authentic Spiritual Values

> *Therefore, confess your sins to each other and pray for each other so that you may be healed. The prayer of a righteous person is powerful and effective.*
> James 5:16

The Epistle of James, one of the 27 books of the New Testament, highlights the significance of communal support and accountability in spiritual growth. In this epistle, James advocates for individuals to acknowledge their weaknesses and pray for one another openly.

This practice is essential in combating hypocrisy, showcasing humility, and accepting imperfections. It promotes spiritual restoration and cultivates genuine community connections.

The Epistle of James underscores the vitality of living out one's faith through action. James not only urges believers to listen to the word of God but also to embody it in their actions. He asserts that faith without action is lifeless and futile. Instead, he underscores the vitality of works in manifesting one's faith and living a righteous life, inspiring believers, and igniting a sense of purpose.

Moreover, the verse affirms that sincere prayer from those living righteously is impactful and profoundly effective. James urges believers to intercede for one another, confess their sins to each other, and seek forgiveness. **He underscores the healing and restorative power of prayer in relationships with God and others**, instilling in believers a sense of hope and reassurance.

Authentic Spiritual Values

The Epistle of James promotes a holistic approach to spiritual growth, emphasizing the importance of faith, action, communal support, and accountability. It encourages believers to live authentic and transparent lives, acknowledging their weaknesses and imperfections and seeking restoration through prayer and community.

Regular Confession

Developing a habit of regular confession can be a powerful tool for personal growth and spiritual development. Admitting your shortcomings to a trusted group of peers creates a safe space for accountability, and support will help you identify areas of weakness and work toward improving them. When choosing the right people to confide in, looking for non-judgmental, compassionate, and trustworthy individuals is essential. You can gain valuable insights into your behavior, thought patterns, and emotional responses by seeking feedback and support from others. Over time, this practice can help you become more self-aware, resilient, and compassionate toward yourself and others.

Intercessory Prayer

Intercessory Prayer is a powerful practice that involves praying for others, especially those facing difficulties situations or challenges. By actively engaging in this practice, you can help foster stronger relationships within your community and promote spiritual growth among all those involved.

Authentic Spiritual Values

Through Intercessory Prayer, you can offer support, comfort, and guidance to those who need it most. This practice allows you to connect with others more profoundly, showing empathy and compassion for their struggles. By lifting others in Prayer, you can create a sense of unity and connectedness within your community, bringing people closer together and strengthening bonds of friendship and faith.

Whether you are praying for a friend, family member, or someone you have never met, Intercessory Prayer can have a powerful impact on both the person receiving the Prayer and those offering it. It can provide comfort, hope, and peace during difficult times and help deepen your spiritual practice and connection with a higher power.

If you want to create a stronger, more connected community and promote spiritual growth among all those involved, consider incorporating Intercessory Prayer into your regular practice. It is a simple yet powerful way to positively impact the lives of those around you and foster a more profound sense of faith and unity within your community.

Embrace Humility

Succeeding in personal and professional settings, embracing humility, and acknowledging your weaknesses are crucial to being honest with yourself and others about areas where you may struggle or not have all the answers. It can be tempting to present a false or hypocritical image, pretending to have all the answers or to be perfect in every way. However, this approach is not only disingenuous but can also lead to missed opportunities for growth and development. Instead, by owning your weaknesses and being open to learning and improvement, you demonstrate a willingness to grow and develop personally and professionally. So, be honest with yourself and those around you, and embrace humility as a critical component of your success.

Create a Prayerful Environment

Create a prayerful environment to foster a culture where prayer is central to community life. Encourage individuals to pray regularly and promote group prayer sessions where members of the Church or community can come together and share their beliefs and experiences. Making prayer a part of everyday life will help individuals develop a deeper connection with their spirituality and feel more connected to their community.

Creating a prayerful environment can promote individual and collective spiritual wellness, helping individuals find peace, comfort, and purpose.

Model Transparency

One practical approach to reduce the stigma around confession and inspire others to do the same is to model transparency. By being open and vulnerable about your struggles and challenges, you set an example for others. Your experiences can help create a culture of openness and acceptance that encourages people to speak up and seek help when needed. This openness can also help to break down the barriers that prevent people from seeking support and reduce the negative attitudes towards those who do. Significantly,

Authentic Spiritual Values

by leading by example and demonstrating vulnerability and openness, you can help to create a more compassionate and supportive community that values honesty, self-reflection, and growth, making everyone feel valued and included.

Chapter Seven

Cultivating Authentic Spiritual Values in Daily Life

The focus is on exploring how the cultivation of genuine spiritual values can be integrated into the church's everyday life. To achieve this, we will undertake an in-depth analysis of scriptural references from the Bible. Our approach will be rooted in the foundational principles underpinning authentic spiritual values, and we aim to emphasize pertinent Biblical passages that illustrate these principles. Ultimately, our objective is to show how the principles can be practically applied within church life to help foster a deeper and more meaningful relationship with God.

> *"Do nothing out of selfish ambition or vain conceit. Rather, in humility, value others above yourselves".*
> Philippians 2:3

Leaders who embody sincere spiritual values can foster stronger bonds of trust and loyalty with their followers. Such leaders are often guided by the teachings of the Bible, which offers valuable insights into the qualities of a good leader. For instance, Philippians 2:3 highlights the importance of humility and selflessness, urging leaders to put the interests of others above their own. Proverbs 3:5-6, on the other hand, encourages leaders to trust in divine guidance and seek wisdom beyond their understanding.

Authentic leadership theory suggests that leaders can significantly enhance their effectiveness by prioritizing transparency, ethics, and self-awareness while remaining grounded in their core values. One practical way for leaders to cultivate authentic spiritual values is through reflective meditation, which promotes self-awareness and aligns personal values with professional actions. Leaders can consistently practice selflessness and humility by daily intending to serve others.

The teachings of Philippians and Proverbs are transformative and provide a comprehensive guide for cultivating authentic spiritual values.

These values, particularly the profound humility nurtured among church leaders, can ignite a powerful transformation within leaders, inspiring them to lead with a more profound sense of purpose and devotion. The teachings emphasize humility and a complete reliance on God rather than one's judgment. In doing so, they seek to encourage leaders to avoid actions driven by selfish desires or pursuing personal glory. Instead, leaders are encouraged to adopt a posture of humility, prioritizing the needs and interests of others above their own. This approach fosters a spirit of service and unity within the church and counters the hypocrisy that can arise from self-centered leadership.

> ***"Trust in the LORD with all your heart.***
> ***And lean not on your understanding;***
> ***In all your ways submit to him,***
> ***And he will* make *your paths straight"*.**
> Proverbs 3:5-6

Authentic Spiritual Values

Leadership is not just about holding a position of power or authority. It's about embodying the spirit of service, selflessness, and humility. Leaders who prioritize the well-being of others above their gain are the ones who genuinely make a difference in the world.

To grow authentically as a spiritual leader, one must adopt a Christ-like servitude that involves putting the needs of others first. This means developing a deeper relationship with God and committing to living out His teachings daily. By acknowledging God's sovereignty and seeking divine guidance in all decisions, leaders can ensure that their path aligns with divine will, thus maintaining integrity and purpose in their leadership.

Leaders who are truly devoted to serving others are not just fulfilling a suggestion, but they are answering a call to action. They recognize that authentic leadership is not about seeking power or recognition but about serving others and fostering a culture of selflessness and unity. By engaging in service within and outside the church, leaders can demonstrate the spirit of Christ's teachings and inspire others to do the same.

Fostering teamwork is a crucial aspect of leadership that requires intentional effort and focus. As a leader, it is essential to encourage collaboration rather than competition among team members and congregants by creating an environment that promotes open communication, mutual respect, and a shared sense of purpose.

Leaders should actively listen to their team members and congregants, showing genuine interest in their thoughts and concerns and demonstrating that their opinions are valued.

In addition to promoting teamwork, personal reflection is also crucial for leaders. They should regularly examine their motivations to ensure they align with serving others rather than individual gain. This can be achieved by practicing self-awareness, reflecting on past decisions and actions, and seeking feedback from others. Leaders should also teach and model humility, using their platform to teach about it and demonstrate it in daily interactions.

Daily devotion is equally significant, and leaders should commit to regular prayer and scripture study to stay connected to God and His guidance. Seeking godly counsel is also an essential aspect of leadership. It is not a sign of weakness but a testament to wisdom and humility. When faced with decisions, consulting with other wise and spiritually mature individuals who can offer godly perspectives and advice is crucial.

It is essential to acknowledge God publicly and regularly credit Him for successes and guidance in ministry, reinforcing His role in all achievements. Leaders should also practice praying for direction before making decisions, emphasizing reliance on God's wisdom. Moreover, leaders should reflect God's will and ensure that all church activities and teachings are aligned with Biblical principles. As a result, they could lead their congregation with integrity, competence, and compassion, fostering a sense of unity and purpose.

Chapter Eight

The Transformative Power of Authenticity in Relationships

This chapter will explore the transformative power of authenticity in building and nurturing a deeper relationship with God. By embracing authenticity, readers can create a more meaningful and genuine connection with the divine, leading to personal growth, spiritual fulfillment, and a greater sense of purpose in life.

Through practical guidance, insightful reflections, and inspiring stories, we will comprehensively explore how authenticity can enrich one's spiritual journey and help them foster a deeper and more fulfilling relationship with God. We will delve into how authenticity can be expressed in one's spiritual practices and beliefs and how it can help individuals discover their true selves and purpose.

We will also explore the challenges one may face on one's journey towards authenticity and how to overcome them. Whether it's overcoming fear, self-doubt, or societal expectations, we will provide practical tips and advice on how one can stay true to oneself and spiritual beliefs, even in adversity?

Overall, this chapter will serve as a comprehensive guide for readers who are looking to deepen their relationship with God and find greater fulfillment in their spiritual journey through the power of authenticity.

> *"Yet to all who did receive him, to those who believed in his name, he gave the right to become children of God."*
> John 1:12

Authenticity is crucial in building meaningful and fulfilling relationships, especially with God. While applying psychological theories such as Attachment theory, Emotional Intelligence, and Interpersonal Neurobiology may seem unconventional in a religious context, they can help us create authentic and responsive interactions that foster deeper connections with God.

As a church community, we are significant in nurturing authenticity in our relationships with God. We are responsible for creating an environment where individuals can feel safe expressing themselves honestly and openly without fear of judgment or rejection. This collective effort is crucial in fostering more profound connections with God.

Emotional intelligence can also help us build more authentic relationships with God. It can help believers better understand and manage their emotions and the emotions of others, communicate more effectively with God, and build deeper connections with Him.

Interpersonal Neurobiology illuminates the transformative potential of authentic relationships with God. This theory underscores how our relationships can shape our brain and nervous system and how we can shape our relationships. Engaging in genuine interactions with God can rewire our

Authentic Spiritual Values

brains, leading to more profound and meaningful connections with Him.

Applying these psychological theories to our daily interactions with God can empower the church community to build stronger relationships with Him.

Attachment theory, we can encourage members to share their personal experiences with God in a safe and non-judgmental environment. This can lead to a more fulfilling spiritual experience characterized by trust, support, and emotional closeness.

> *"Therefore, if anyone is in Christ, the new creation has come:[a] The old has gone, the new is here!"*.
> 2 Corinthians 5:17

Emotional Intelligence (EI) is a set of abilities that involves recognizing and understanding our emotions and those of others. It enables us to navigate social situations with greater ease and sensitivity, fostering authenticity and deeper connections in our relationships with faith. By developing our EI, we can better understand our motivations and desires and those of God, leading to a more profound sense of purpose and fulfillment in our spiritual journey.

Interpersonal Neurobiology (IPNB) is an interdisciplinary field that explores the connection between our brain and our relationships. It highlights the profound impact of authentic interactions on our brain and nervous system.

Engaging in genuine interactions with God and other church community members stimulates neural pathways associated with trust, connection, and emotional regulation to create a more profound sense of fulfillment in our relationships with God.

By cultivating our EI and engaging in authentic interactions with God and other church members, we can experience a more profound connection with our faith and a greater sense of purpose and fulfillment in our spiritual journey; this enhances our well-being and makes life more meaningful and fulfilling.

Interpersonal Neurobiology Theory

Interpersonal neurobiology theory is a fascinating perspective that sheds light on the transformative potential of authentic relationships with God. This theory posits that our relationships are deeply interconnected and can profoundly impact our brain and nervous system. By cultivating authenticity in our spiritual practices and connections with others, we can deepen our relationship with God and experience significant growth and fulfillment on our spiritual journey.

Interpersonal neurobiology theory provides a framework for understanding how genuine relationships with God can shape our spiritual experiences, brains, and nervous systems. This theory suggests that we can cultivate a deep and meaningful relationship by actively fostering authenticity in our spiritual practices and connections with others and relationship with God to bring about profound change and growth.

The theory highlights the importance of cultivating authentic relationships with God and others and how these relationships can help us navigate the complexities of life with greater ease and purpose.

Brain Plasticity and Spiritual Practices

Interpersonal neurobiology is a field that has identified the brain's remarkable ability to change and adapt in response to experiences, a phenomenon known as "brain plasticity." Regarding spiritual practices, research has shown that engaging in prayer, meditation, and worship can stimulate neural pathways associated with positive emotions, spiritual connection, and overall well-being. This means that through regular participation in these practices, individuals can promote neural changes that deepen their relationship with God and foster spiritual growth.

It's important to note, however, that the effectiveness of these practices depends on cultivating authenticity and sincerity in them. By doing so, individuals can maximize the potential for positive neural changes that enhance their spiritual lives.

Authentic Spiritual Values

> ***You have been born again, not of perishable seed, but of imperishable, through God's living and enduring word.***
> 1 Peter 1:23

Attachment theory is a crucial component of interpersonal neurobiology that suggests individuals form attachment bonds with others and God. Being sincere and transparent in prayer, worship, and spiritual dialogue is essential to forging an authentic relationship with God. A secure attachment to God is characterized by trust, intimacy, and emotional connection, which can provide security and comfort, even in times of difficulty or uncertainty.

Interpersonal neurobiology highlights the crucial role of relationships in regulating emotions and promoting emotional well-being. Authenticity in relationships with God can lead to profound spiritual experiences characterized by peace, joy, and a sense of transcendence.

These experiences calm the nervous system, promoting emotional resilience and spiritual fulfillment. In other words, spiritual experiences can help people regulate their emotions, fostering a sense of calm and inner peace, leading to emotional stability and enhanced well-being.

> **"Peter replied, "Repent and be baptized, every one of you, in the name of Jesus Christ for the forgiveness of your sins. And you will receive the gift of the Holy Spirit".**
> Acts 2:38

Interpersonal neurobiology, a field that explores how our social connections impact our mental and emotional health, underscores the significance of social support and spiritual community for individuals seeking spiritual growth. Authentic relationships built upon shared faith and a typical journey can provide a sense of belonging, encouragement, and support essential for nurturing one's mental and emotional well-being. By fostering genuine connections with others who share their faith journey; individuals can deepen their relationship with God and experience the transformative power of community.

The spiritual community provides a safe space for individuals to share their struggles, hopes, and dreams and to receive guidance and support from others who have walked similar paths. The bonds formed within these communities can be a source of great strength and comfort, helping individuals weather life's storms and grow in their spiritual journey.

Emotional intelligence theory

Emotional intelligence theory provides a framework for understanding how being true to Relationships with God can have a transformative effect by leading to self-awareness, emotional regulation, empathy, and social connection. For instance, by recognizing and understanding our emotions, we can better understand the messages God may be sending us through our feelings. By cultivating emotional intelligence in their spiritual lives, individuals can deepen their relationship with God and experience profound growth and fulfillment on their spiritual journey. Emotional intelligence theory offers insights into recognizing, understanding, and managing emotions, as well as acknowledging and empathizing with the feelings of others.

At the core of emotional intelligence lies self-awareness, the key to recognizing and understanding our emotions. In our relationships with God, authenticity is paramount. This authenticity requires a deep self-awareness of our beliefs, doubts, fears, and desires. To truly express our thoughts and feelings to God, we must cultivate self-awareness, strengthen our spiritual connection, and foster personal growth.

Emotional regulation, a crucial component of emotional intelligence, empowers us to manage our emotions effectively. In our authentic relationships with God, expressing emotions such as gratitude, love, doubt, and even anger is vital to healthy and constructive. By practicing emotional regulation in our spiritual lives, we can develop spiritual resilience, navigating challenges and setbacks with grace and unwavering trust in God's guidance.

Empathy is a fundamental aspect of emotional intelligence that is crucial in building authentic relationships with God and others. It refers to the ability to understand and share the feelings of others, putting oneself in their shoes and seeing things from their perspective. In doing so, one can extend compassion and love to those in need, creating deeper connections and fostering a sense of unity and mutual understanding.

To cultivate empathy in their spiritual lives, individuals can start by listening attentively to others and trying to understand their experiences without judgment. They can also practice self-reflection and awareness, acknowledging their emotions and how they may impact their interactions. By doing so, they can develop further empathy and compassion in their relationships create a more supportive and loving community.

Social Awareness

Social awareness is another crucial aspect of emotional intelligence for building authentic relationships with God and others. It involves recognizing and understanding the emotions and needs of others within a social context, such as a spiritual community. By fostering social awareness, individuals can build genuine connections with others who share their faith journey, finding support, encouragement, and shared spiritual growth.

To develop social awareness, one can start by paying attention to others' emotions and behaviors and understanding their perspectives and needs.

They can also engage in active listening and communication, expressing empathy and compassion for others' experiences. By doing so, they can create a more supportive and inclusive community that fosters spiritual growth and transformation.

Conflict Resolution and Forgiveness

These are also essential skills for emotional intelligence, particularly in authentic relationships with God. Seeking reconciliation and forgiveness with oneself and others is a crucial aspect of spiritual growth, allowing individuals to heal from past wounds and move forward in their faith journey.

To practice conflict resolution and forgiveness, individuals can start by acknowledging their role in conflicts and seeking to understand others' perspectives. They can also practice forgiveness and compassion, extending grace and mercy to others and themselves. They can experience healing and transformation, deepen their relationship with God and others, and create a more loving and supportive community.

Attachment Theory

Attachment theory is a well-established psychological framework that seeks to explain how individuals form attachment bonds with other people and authority figures, including God. As per the theory, relationships with God can be crucial to one's overall emotional and psychological well-being. Attachment theory suggests cultivating authenticity in one's relationship with God can be transformative, leading to profound growth, healing, and fulfillment on one's spiritual journey.

The concept of secure attachment to God is central to attachment theory. Just like individuals seek security and comfort in attachment relationships with caregivers, they also seek a sense of security and connection with God. When one has a secure attachment to God, they experience trust, intimacy, and emotional connection that can provide a sense of security and comfort, even in times of difficulty or uncertainty.

Authentic Spiritual Values

Authenticity in relationships with God involves being genuine, sincere, and transparent in one's prayers, worship, and spiritual practices.

By cultivating authenticity in their relationship with God, individuals can experience deeper intimacy and trust, leading to healthy relational models that foster secure attachment bonds, emotional regulation, exploration, growth, and healing. Attachment theory provides a valuable framework for understanding how authenticity in relationships with God can contribute to one's overall emotional and

Psychological well-being: By seeking a sense of security and connection in their relationship with God and cultivating authenticity in their spiritual practices, individuals can experience profound growth, healing, and fulfillment on their spiritual journey.

Attachment theory suggests that individuals establish attachment bonds with significant others who act as comfort and regulation sources during stress and distress. However, when these attachment figures are unavailable or fail to provide the desired emotional support, cultivating authentic relationships with God can be a potent source of emotional comfort and support. This can aid individuals in regulating their emotions and finding solace in times of need, offering a unique and potentially beneficial avenue for emotional well-being.

Prayer, meditation, and other spiritual practices are not just individual endeavors but powerful tools for fostering a sense of community and connection with God. When individuals approach God sincerely, they can experience the transformative effects of spiritual comfort and emotional regulation. Research has demonstrated that prayer and other forms of spiritual engagement can alleviate symptoms of anxiety and depression, boost well-being, and foster a deep sense of connection with others and the Divine. This sense of community offers tangible benefits, making it a powerful source of support and belonging for those who engage in these practices.

Attachment theory also underscores the significance of secure attachment relationships in encouraging exploration and development. In a relationship with God, individuals can delve into their beliefs, questions, doubts, and spiritual experiences within a secure and supportive environment. This can lead to substantial personal and spiritual growth, deepening one's relationship with God and broadening one's self-understanding and understanding of the divine, providing a psychological framework for one's spiritual journey.

However, it is essential to note that early attachment experiences can shape individuals' relational patterns and emotional well-being, affecting their ability to trust, connect, and experience intimacy authentically. Individuals may bring attachment wounds or insecurities into their relationship with God, which can hinder their ability to experience God's love gracefully. Nevertheless, through authentic engagement with God and spiritual practices, individuals can experience healing and transformation, finding healing for past attachment wounds and developing secure attachment bonds with God.

Authentic Spiritual Values

Attachment theory, a psychological framework, posits that individuals develop internalized models of relationships based on their early attachment experiences. These models influence their expectations and behaviors in future relationships. However, the transformative power of authentic relationships with God cannot be overstated. Such relationships can reshape one's relational models, fostering greater trust, security, and intimacy in relationships with God and others. Genuine spiritual experiences and encounters with the divine can revolutionize these models, significantly deepening one's capacity for intimacy and connection in all areas of life.

Matthew 23:25-27, a chapter that starkly contrasts superficial or hypocritical interactions with authentic relationships based on sincerity, vulnerability, trust, and integrity, further underscores this point. Encouraging individuals to be open and share their true selves with others fosters trust and nurtures emotional intimacy in their relationships.

Communication skills

The process of effective communication is challenging, especially when it comes to conveying one's true feelings and thoughts. However, individuals can learn to communicate more effectively by promoting authenticity through active listening, assertiveness, and empathy. In addition, it is essential to explore the concept of boundaries and authenticity in relationships, as setting healthy boundaries can help individuals honor their authentic needs and values while respecting the autonomy of others involves understanding the importance of maintaining a balance between one's own needs and desires and those of others within the context of a relationship. By doing so, individuals can create healthier and more fulfilling relationships based on mutual respect and understanding.

Conflict resolution

The experts offer comprehensive strategies for positively, constructively, and authentically handling conflicts. They emphasize the importance of honesty, empathy, and a willingness to compromise as critical elements in resolving disputes and building healthy relationships. By using these strategies allow individuals to navigate complex situations and communicate their needs more effectively.

The experts encourage individuals to cultivate self-awareness and reflect on their relational patterns and dynamics. This includes examining their behaviors and attitudes in relationships and recognizing areas where they may be acting in-authentically or perpetuating unhealthy patterns. By becoming more aware of these patterns, individuals can change their behavior and create healthier, more fulfilling relationships.

Chapter Nine

Lessons from Jesus' Teachings on Authenticity

The chapter "Lessons from Jesus' Teachings on Authenticity" is a thought-provoking and insightful piece of literature that delves into Jesus Christ's profound insights about authenticity and genuine spirituality. The chapter is based on various passages from the Bible and offers an in-depth exploration of critical lessons essential for anyone on a spiritual journey. It is an excellent resource that provides practical insights and biblical truths that inspire readers to pursue authentic living and cultivate a genuine relationship with God.

The chapter offers a detailed analysis of Jesus' teachings about authenticity and genuine spirituality, highlighting the importance of honesty, integrity, and transparency in one's spiritual journey. It provides a comprehensive understanding of the central theme of Jesus' teachings, which is the importance of being true to oneself and others. The chapter explores authenticity aspects, such as self-awareness, self-acceptance, and self-expression, and offers practical tips and advice for cultivating these qualities.

The chapter also highlights the importance of developing a genuine relationship with God based on trust, love, and faith. It offers a detailed examination of how one can cultivate a meaningful and authentic relationship with God and provides practical strategies for deepening one's spiritual life. With its timeless wisdom and valuable insights, this chapter is an ideal resource for anyone looking to deepen their spiritual journey and pursue a life of authenticity and genuine spirituality.

Basis in Scripture

This chapter is centered around the teachings of Jesus Christ, as recorded in the Gospel accounts of Matthew, Mark, Luke, and John. These texts provide valuable insights into the concept of authenticity in spirituality. One of the central passages is Matthew 23:25-27, in which Jesus criticizes the hypocrisy of the Pharisees and emphasizes the importance of sincerity and truthfulness in one's spiritual journey. Furthermore, the Sermon on the Mount (Matthew 5-7) is another crucial text that contributes to our understanding of authenticity and guides how to live an authentic life. Jesus' interactions with his followers also offer value perspectives on authenticity, such as his emphasis on love, forgiveness, and humility.

By exploring Jesus's teachings, we can understand what it means to live an authentic spiritual life and how to cultivate sincerity and truthfulness in our thoughts, words, and actions.

Key Concepts

This chapter delves into two critical aspects of spirituality that Jesus emphasized during his time on earth. The first is the contrast between authenticity and hypocrisy, a recurring theme in the Gospels. Jesus challenged the religious authorities of his day, who engaged in superficial displays of piety but lacked genuine faith and inner transformation. He called for his followers to lead authentic lives characterized by integrity and sincerity in their spiritual journey.

The second aspect of spirituality that Jesus emphasized is the importance of inner transformation and heart change. He taught that true spirituality is not just about external rituals and observances but purity of heart and genuine devotion to God. This chapter explores how deepening one's relationship with God can lead to profound inner transformation and spiritual growth. It highlights how Jesus' teachings on inner transformation are still relevant today and how they can inspire us to live more meaningful and fulfilling lives.

The teachings and way of life of Jesus Christ serve as a radiant beacon of radical love and compassion for humanity, and the notion that genuine spirituality can be best embodied when nurturing a deep passion for both God and one's fellow human beings, as exemplified by Jesus' commandment to love each other as he has loved us (John 13:34-35).

To embody the essence of authentic spirituality, one must demonstrate selfless service, empathy, and compassion toward others. Just as Jesus lived a life of unconditional love and generosity, believers can only attain it through a sincere desire to serve others and positively impact the world around them. As Jesus himself said in the book of Matthew 5:13-14. This highlights the importance of leading a life of purpose, compassion, and service, bringing joy, hope, and light to the world, and remaining faithful to our calling as followers of Jesus Christ.

"You are the light of the world. A town built on a hill cannot be hidden. ¹⁵ Neither do people light a lamp and put it under a bowl. Instead, they put it on its stand, giving everyone in the house light. ¹⁶ In the same way, let your light shine before others, that they may see your good deeds and glorify your Father in heaven."
Matthew 5: 13-14.

Practical Applications:

The book in question is a compelling and thought-provoking work that delves into authenticity and its importance in the spiritual lives of those who aspire to follow Jesus' teachings. The author emphasizes that true and profound transformation can only occur when individuals engage in self-examination and introspection, enabling them to identify insincerity or hypocrisy in their spiritual lives.

The chapter highlights the significance of cultivating a deep and authentic relationship with God. The author stresses the importance of sincere prayer, worship, and faith, grounded in a profound love and reverence for the divine. Drawing on Jesus' example, the readers are encouraged to develop a deeply personal and genuine.

Connection with God is marked by honesty, vulnerability, and authenticity. Furthermore, the book provides practical insights on how to live out one's authenticity daily. The author emphasizes the importance of reflecting on the values of the kingdom of God in one's relationships, work, and community involvement as the key to demonstrating authenticity and positively impacting the world.

Authentic Spiritual Values

The teachings of Jesus on authenticity are explored in depth, and readers will understand how these teachings remain relevant to modern-day spiritual seekers. By internalizing these teachings and imbibing them daily, readers can learn to live authentically and positively impact those around them. The book is a must-read for anyone seeking to deepen their spiritual life, cultivate an authentic relationship with God, and positively impact the world through their actions and values.

"Do not store up for yourselves treasures on earth, where moths and vermin destroy, and where thieves break in and steal. [20] But store up for yourselves treasures in heaven, where moths and vermin do not destroy, and Where thieves do not break in and steal. [21] For where your treasure is, there your heart will be also.". 6: 19-21.

Jesus Christ's teachings are a powerful guide and inspiration for the Church and people worldwide. One of the most profound aspects of his teachings is his emphasis on authenticity and sincerity. Jesus encouraged his followers to embrace their authentic selves and live in a way aligned with their deepest values and beliefs. This path of authenticity can be transformative, leading to a deeper connection with the divine and a more fulfilling spiritual life.

The chapter highlighting Jesus' teachings invites readers to draw inspiration from his example and apply his teachings to their everyday lives. The chapter emphasizes the personal journey of embracing sincerity, integrity, and love in one's spiritual walk. It encourages individuals to reflect on their innermost thoughts and feelings and align them with their actions. By doing so, people can cultivate a sense of personal

Authentic Spiritual Values

involvement in their spiritual growth rather than simply conforming to societal expectations or other people's opinions.

The teachings in this chapter offer practical guidance for living a life of authenticity and sincerity. For example, individuals are encouraged to be honest with themselves about their strengths and weaknesses and to work on developing their character in a way consistent with their values. The Church was instructed to be kind and compassionate to others, treating them with the same respect and understanding as they would like to receive. Ultimately, the teachings of Jesus Christ offer a powerful path for those seeking to live a life of purpose, meaning, and connection to the divine.

Living authentically is crucial for our spiritual growth and plays a significant role in positively impacting the world around us.

This chapter emphasizes the importance of living authentically and making a positive difference in the lives of others. It encourages individuals to utilize their unique gifts, talents, and experiences to serve others, improve the world, and lead purposeful and meaningful lives.

The teachings on authenticity offer a practical and profound way to connect with the divine and fulfill our life's purpose. We can discover our true selves by aligning our actions, beliefs, and values with our inherent nature and find our place in the world. This process of self-discovery and self-realization enables us to live fulfilling and purposeful lives while positively impacting the lives of those around us.

Living authentically enables us to be present, honest, and sincere in our interactions. It allows us to cultivate meaningful relationships based on trust, respect, and understanding. Furthermore, authenticity empowers us to embrace our imperfections, vulnerabilities, and challenges, ultimately leading to personal growth and transformation.

Authenticity is vital to our personal and spiritual growth and offers a practical and meaningful way to connect with our higher selves and the world around us. By following the teachings on authenticity, we can live an authentic life to our nature, serve others, and positively impact the world.

Chapter Ten

Reflections on Personal Authenticity and Spiritual Development

I have sought solace and wisdom in the teachings of God. One of the significant passage I read most I Colossians 3:12, which comes from a letter written by Apostle Paul to the Colossian church. In this verse, Paul exhorts the Colossians to live a life transformed by their faith in Jesus Christ. This verse serves as a guide for me, illustrating how to embody traits that align with the values of this new life in Christ and move away from the ways of the past characterized by sin. I interpret this transformation as a fundamental shift in mindset and behavior, and Colossians 3:12 provides a roadmap for this remarkable change.

Apostle Paul's message to the Colossian Christians profoundly resonates with my transformation journey. In his letter, he exhorts them to live lives that reflect the worthiness of their calling as followers of Christ. He explicitly outlines negative behaviors that they should discard, including anger, malice, and slander (Colossians 3:8). These vices are not mentioned haphazardly but rather as specific stumbling blocks that can impede our spiritual development and harm our relationships.

For instance, unrestrained anger can lead to hurtful words and destructive actions, while harboring malice and engaging in slanderous behavior can erode trust and unity within a community. Recognizing and acknowledging these behaviors constituted the initial step in my journey toward personal transformation and spiritual growth.

> *"Therefore, as God's chosen people, holy and dearly loved, clothe yourselves with compassion, kindness, humility, gentleness, and patience."*
> Colossians 3:12

The concept of "clothing themselves" in the Bible goes beyond mere physical dressing. It signifies a deliberate adoption of new virtues, a transformation in one's mindset, and a change in one's fundamental ideas. Just like we carefully select our attire when visiting essential figures such as a king, a politician, or respected in-laws, "clothing ourselves" suggests choosing virtues and values to align with the occasion. When we dress appropriately for an occasion, we experience a sense of confidence, boldness, and happiness. This analogy encourages us to "clothe" ourselves with the virtues and values of GOD daily. These virtues are not inherently ingrained within us but require us to seek and uphold them actively.

Incorporating new virtues such as compassion, kindness, humility, gentleness, and patience is not just something I consider in theory; it is a practical and tangible way for me to embody the nature of Christ. As a Christian, I choose to embody these characteristics because they reflect the expected behavior of Christians. "Born Again" is not merely a label to me; it signifies genuine Christian faith, demonstrated through practical and relational actions towards others and the world around us.

Authentic Spiritual Values

Colossians 3:12 provides a blueprint for this outward expression of inward faith.

Compassion and Kindness

The traits mentioned in the passage exemplify a deep sense of compassion and empathy toward the suffering and needs of others. Genuine faith empowers individuals to connect with and understand the struggles of others, compelling them to provide tangible assistance and emotional support. For example, one might be moved by compassion to dedicate time to volunteering at a local shelter, offering aid to those in need. Similarly, kindness may inspire someone to lend a supportive and attentive ear to a friend facing challenges, demonstrating care and empathy in a meaningful way.

Humility

Humility in faith involves actively resisting the pride and self-centeredness that often characterize human nature. By practicing humility, individuals acknowledge their limitations and embrace their dependence on God. This mindset enables them to enhance their capacity for serving others without seeking personal recognition or glory, as they prioritize the well-being and needs of others over their desires.

Gentleness and Patience

This set of personal characteristics profoundly influences one's response to provocation and adversity. Cultivating gentleness, tempering reactions, and exercising patience enable individuals to adopt a long-suffering attitude toward others' faults. These traits are paramount in fostering and sustaining harmonious relationships with God and others.

Broader Biblical Integration

Paul's exhortation to embrace these virtues resonates with other New Testament teachings, particularly the description of the fruits of the Spirit in Galatians 5:22-23. Moreover, Jesus' own life and teachings are a profound embodiment of these qualities—illustrated by his compassion for the multitudes, his humility in washing the disciples' feet, his gentle approach to sinners, and his enduring patience during times of trial.

Colossians 3:12 weaves a rich tapestry of virtues, guiding us toward authentic Christian behavior. This passage calls us to action and presents a compelling challenge to construct communities that actively mirror the grace and righteousness of the kingdom of God.

The Authenticity Inherent

The contemplation of authenticity and spiritual development, individuals can embark on a journey of self-discovery and personal growth that ultimately leads to a more fulfilling life. This path encourages individuals to connect with their true selves, live by their highest values and principles, and attain greater wholeness and authenticity. It fosters personal transformation and deepens one's understanding of oneself and our world.

Living an authentic life involves embracing vulnerability and revealing our true selves without masks or pretenses. It means being courageous enough to show our imperfections and unique qualities to ourselves, others, and the divine.

Authenticity is also about living in a way aligned with our values, beliefs, and convictions. It requires us to stay true to ourselves and strive for integrity, even when it's not the easiest or most popular choice. We can experience a deep sense of unity and inner peace when we act on our inner truths.

Additionally, authenticity demands that we listen to and honor our inner voice. This small voice of intuition and conscience guides us toward living by our deepest values and truths. By following this guidance, we can cultivate a rich life with purpose, meaning, and fulfillment.

Embracing Growth and Change

Authenticity is a profoundly transformative and empowering process involving an ongoing journey of self-discovery and personal growth. It is a call to embrace change, to allow ourselves to evolve and develop mentally, emotionally, and spiritually. The journey towards authenticity is a challenging one. We may encounter challenges, setbacks, and moments of uncertainty that could leave us feeling lost and disillusioned. However, these experiences are not roadblocks; they can be viewed as steppingstones that offer valuable learning opportunities and help us grow and transform personally. By facing our fears and embracing change, we can unlock our full potential and discover our true selves, leading to a more fulfilling and authentic life.

Cultivating Compassion and Acceptance

Authenticity is a multi-faceted concept that entails accepting our humanity entirely, including the parts we may perceive as flawed, weak, or mistaken. However, it's about accepting and doing so with kindness and understanding. When we approach our flaws with compassion and empathy, we create a safe space for genuine self-expression and growth for ourselves and others around us. This fosters an environment of acceptance and understanding, promoting personal growth and positive change.

In addition, authenticity is a crucial aspect of spiritual development, which involves deepening our connection with the divine through genuine and sincere practices such as prayer, meditation, reflection, and worship. Engaging in these practices with authenticity and deep intention allows us to nurture our spiritual connection and develop a stronger relationship with the divine. It enables us to tap into the wisdom and guidance of the universe and align our actions with our values and beliefs, leading to a greater sense of purpose and fulfillment in life. Therefore, authenticity is a way of being and a path to spiritual awakening and enlightenment.

Authenticity is essential to personal growth and development, and genuine relationships are crucial. When we cultivate authentic relationships, we build a safe environment where we can be honest and vulnerable and trust each other.

Authentic Spiritual Values

Such relationships provide us with the support and guidance we need to navigate our respective journeys and learn from one another.

By being true to ourselves and our values, we can live with purpose and meaning, another vital aspect of authenticity. When we align with our authentic selves, we can better discern our purpose in life and live accordingly. This leads to a more fulfilling and satisfying life, where we engage in meaningful pursuits that align with our true selves and contribute to our personal growth.

Living authentically brings a deep sense of fulfillment and satisfaction as we connect with our true selves and the world around us. It allows us to become more aware of our thoughts, feelings, and behaviors and make conscious choices that align with our values and beliefs. This, in turn, leads to a greater sense of purpose and satisfaction in life.

Chapter Eleven

Conclusion: Embracing Authenticity in Pursuit of Spiritual Wholeness

"The Authentic Spiritual Value" is an incredible guidebook that delves deep into the importance of embracing authenticity to achieve spiritual wholeness. The book comprehensively explains spirituality and how individuals can align their values and beliefs to achieve spiritual development. It is an essential read for anyone seeking to deepen their spiritual journey by living authentically by their actual values and beliefs and recognizing this as a critical element of spiritual growth.

The book highlights the significance of prioritizing authenticity to strengthen our connection with our spiritual selves, cultivate a greater sense of inner peace, and engage more meaningfully with the world. The author explains that when we align our actions with our values and beliefs, we feel more fulfilled, satisfied, and at peace with ourselves. Living authentically can be a powerful tool in promoting spiritual growth and fulfillment.

The book's conclusion reinforces these key themes, emphasizing the transformative power of living authentically to promote spiritual growth and fulfillment. It offers practical advice and actionable steps to help individuals live authentically and lead more fulfilling lives.

Authentic Spiritual Values

The book is a valuable resource for anyone exploring spirituality and seeking inner peace. It provides detailed insights and guidance on aligning one's values and beliefs with one's actions to achieve spiritual development and, ultimately, a sense of fulfillment and peace.

Authentic Spiritual Values

Chapter Twelve

Overcoming Hypocrisy: The Salvation VS Cathedrals. (FIG TREE)

It is a matter of concern that some church leaders prioritize financial gain over genuine spiritual guidance, which can lead to a distorted view of the church's purpose. This can create a dangerous notion that a church's size indicates divine favor.

To understand the true purpose and organization of the church, we can turn to God's instructions to Moses, which clearly explain the church's role and function. By studying these principles in-depth, church leaders can identify practical steps to steer the church back onto a path that aligns with the scriptural foundations of the faith.

Church leaders should prioritize genuine spiritual guidance over financial gain and focus on the principles that the faith is built upon rather than equating success with the size of their congregation. By doing so, they can ensure that the church remains true to its purpose and faithfully serves its members. This approach will lead to a healthier and more spiritually fulfilling church community.

Authentic Spiritual Values

Chapter Thirteen

References and Further Study

"The Cost of Discipleship" by Dietrich Bonhoeffer - This book delves into the concept of "cheap grace" versus "costly grace," advocating for a Christianity that goes beyond superficial faith, akin to the deeper spiritual purity Jesus demands in Matthew 23:25.

"The Wounded Healer" by Henri Nouwen-Nouwen discusses how spiritual leaders must acknowledge their vulnerabilities and imperfections to authentically minister to others, resonating with the call to internal purity in Matthew 23:25.

Pao, D. (2014). Let No One Despise Your Youth: Church and The World in The Pastoral Epistles. Journal of the Evangelical Theological Society, 57(4), 743-755.

The Enchanting Essence of Emotional Beauty - Welcome to Hogaplus.com - Change the Lifestyle.
https://hogaplus.com/the-enchanting-essence-of-emotional-beauty/

Colophon

Colophon for "Authentic Spiritual Values": A comprehensive guide to understanding and embracing spiritual principles in the modern world.

This book, Authentic Spiritual Values, was completed in June 2024 and printed and bound by Amazon.com,.inc Digital, North Seattle. It spans [number of pages] and the text is set in Garamond, a classic serif typeface originally designed by Claude Garamond in the 16th century, chosen for its readability and elegance, reflecting the timeless and contemplative nature of the book's content.

The paper used for this edition is Fine Mark Cream, a high-quality, acid-free paper known for its durability and excellent ink holdout. This ensures that each page maintains its integrity over time. Fine Mark Cream is sourced from responsibly managed forests, underscoring our commitment to environmental sustainability.

H. Town Printing and Bindery Services Inc. created the cover design, which features an abstract representation of spiritual growth. The cover utilizes a soft matte finish with embossed lettering to provide a tactile experience, enhancing the physical engagement with the book.

Authentic Spiritual Values was meticulously edited by Rev. Dr. OVGeart, whose insightful feedback and meticulous attention to detail significantly shaped the final manuscript. I and Rev. Dr. OVGeart performed the layout and typesetting, bringing clarity and aesthetic harmony to the

Authentic Spiritual Values

text's presentation, a testament to our dedication to delivering a high-quality reading experience.

This book is published in hardcover and softcover to ensure durability and a lasting presence in readers' libraries. It is also available in a convenient digital format, compatible with all major e-readers. It offers adjustable typesetting features to cater to personal reading preferences, making it accessible to readers wherever they are.

ISBN: 979-889480729-4

Tagline:
"Discover the transformative power of authenticity on your spiritual journey."

Blurb:

Amidst a world filled with superficiality and pretense, "Authentic Spiritual Values" presents a compelling perspective on what it truly means to lead a spiritually fulfilling life. Drawing inspiration from both timeless wisdom traditions and modern insights, this book serves as a guiding light for readers on the path of self-discovery and inner transformation.

Through captivating narratives, thought-provoking reflections, and practical exercises, "Authentic Spiritual Values" delves into the essence of authenticity in spirituality. From exploring the teachings of Jesus on integrity and sincerity to embracing the principles of mindfulness and self-awareness, readers are encouraged to embark on a journey of self-discovery and uncover the authentic truths that reside within them.

Whether one aims to deepen their connection with the divine, nurture meaningful relationships, or discover more significant purpose and fulfillment, "Authentic Spiritual Values" provides invaluable guidance and inspiration for the journey ahead. It's a call to embrace one's true self, align with one's deepest values, and revel in the profound joy of living authentically.

Authentic Spiritual Values

Testimonials:

"Authentic Spiritual Values":

1. "A beautifully written and deeply insightful exploration of authenticity in spirituality. This book has the power to transform lives and awaken hearts to the truth of who we are."

2. "Authentic Spiritual Values provides a refreshing perspective in a world filled with spiritual noise. Its message of authenticity resonates deeply and offers a much-needed reminder of what truly matters in our spiritual journey."

3. "As a spiritual teacher, I've delved into numerous books on spirituality, but Authentic Spiritual Values shines as a gem. Its wisdom is timeless, its insights profound, and its guidance practical. I wholeheartedly recommend it to anyone seeking a deeper connection with themselves and the divine."

First Edition

For further information about Authentic Spiritual Values or to order additional copies, contact us at authenticspiritualvalue@gmail.com

We hope this book offers profound insights and enriching reflections on your spiritual journey.

Other Books to Watch Out for from the Author:

- ❖ Sanctuary of Shadows
- ❖ Choices at Crossroad. Etc.